Napoleon and Josephine

"His wife Josephine had given him anxiety during the Italian expedition. To his ardent and desperate love-letters she had replied, he said, as though she were a woman of fifty. In Egypt he obtained proof of her infidelity; and the whole experience in the mind of so earnest a lover, produced a distress which a biographer must not fail to note. He thought of divorce: he wrote to his brother:

The veil is completely torn away. . . . I am weary of human nature, and grandeur is only a burden to me. Feeling has withered; glory has become stale; at 29 I have drunk life to the dregs. There is nothing left for me now but to become a complete egoist.

. . . . And when on his return to France his step-children interceded for Josephine, he took her back into his affections; for he could not resist their tears."

—from Chapter II

NAPOLEON

Herbert Butterfield

COLLIER BOOKS

NEW YORK

First published in 1939. Reprinted 1940, 1947, 1957. First published in the United States in 1956. All Rights Reserved. Napoleon was published in a hardcover edition by The Macmillan Company. The Macmillan Company, New York. Printed in the United States of America. First Collier Books Edition 1962.

THIRD PRINTING 1966

FOR
WICKY

Contents

Chronological Table

1769	Aug. 15	Birth
1779	April	Admitted to military school of Brienne
1784	Oct.	Military school at Paris
1785-7		Artillery Officer at Valence
1787-91		At Auxonne
1789		*French Revolution*
1792-3		Activity in Corsica
1793	Dec.	At the Siege of Toulon
1794	Feb.	Appointed General in Command of the Artillery of the Army of Italy
	July 27	Fall of Robespierre
1795	Aug. 22	*Establishment of the Directory*
	Oct. 4	Suppresses revolt in Paris
1796	March 9	Marries Josephine de Beauharnais
1796-7		Campaign of Italy
1797	April 18	Preliminaries of Leoben
	Sept. 4	Coup d'état of 18 Fructidor
	Oct. 17	Treaty of Campo-Formio
1798-9		Egyptian expedition
1798	Aug.	Battle of the Nile
1799	March-May	Siege of Acre
	April	Renewal of coalition against France
	Oct. 8	Bonaparte lands in France
	Nov. 9-10	*Coup d'état of 18-19 Brumaire*
1800	June 14	Battle of Marengo
1801	Feb. 9	Treaty of Lunéville
	July 15	The Concordat with the Papacy
1802	Mar. 27	Treaty of Amiens
	Aug. 15	Consul for Life
	Sept. 21	Incorporation of Piedmont in France

1803	Feb. 19	Act of Mediation constituting the Swiss Confederation
	May 18	Rupture of the Peace of Amiens
1804	Mar.	The Civil Code
		Cadoudal's conspiracy
	Mar. 21	Execution of the Duc d'Enghien
	May	*Napoleon becomes Emperor*
	Dec.	Coronation
1805	May	King of Italy
1805		*War of the Third Coalition*
	Oct. 17	Capitulation of Ulm
	Oct 21	Trafalgar
	Dec. 2	Austerlitz
1806		War with Prussia
	Oct. 14	Battle of Jena
	Nov. 21	Berlin Decree
1807	June 14	Battle of Friedland
	July 7	Treaty of Tilsit
	Oct.-Nov.	French invasion of Portugal
1808		Expedition to Spain
	Oct.	Meeting with Czar at Erfurt
1809	March	War with Austria
	May	Annexation of the Papal States
	Dec. 15	Divorce of Josephine
1810	April	Marriage with Marie Louise of Austria
	July	Holland annexed to the French Empire
1811	Mar. 20	Birth of a son, the King of Rome
1812	June 22	*War with Russia*
	July 22	Battle of Salamanca
	Sept. 7	Battle of Borodino
	Sept. 14	Entry into Moscow
	Oct. 19	Departure from Moscow
	Oct. 23	Battle at Malayaroslavetz
	Nov. 26-28	Passage of the Beresina

1813	Feb. 27	Prussia allies with Russia in the Treaty of Kalisch
	Aug. 10	Austria at war with France
	Oct. 18-19	Battle of the Nations at Leipzig
1814	Mar. 31	Surrender of Paris
	April 14	*First abdication of Napoleon*
	Sept.	Congress of Vienna meets
1815	Feb. 26	Napoleon leaves Elba
	March 20	Reaches Paris
	March 25	Outlawed by the Powers
	June 18	Waterloo
	June 22	*Second abdication*
	Oct. 17	Arrives in St. Helena
1821	May 5	Death of Napoleon
1840	Dec. 15	Removal of his remains to Paris

Napoleon

Chapter 1

Introduction

THE "principles of 1789" sprang from a philosophy so liberal, an enthusiasm so sympathetically human— and the rights of men were so trumpeted in the early days of the French Revolution—that Mazzini was able to look upon this period of history as a fulfilment of Christianity, the triumph of individualism. It is strange, therefore—it is a comment on the wayward- ness of our historical development—that the Revo- lution itself should have quickly produced an engine more dreadful than any of the absolute monarchs had had at their command for the repression of the indi- vidual, inaugurating a type of polity more formidable as an organ of power than ancient feudalisms and ill-jointed dynastic systems could ever have hoped to achieve. Beginning with views much too doctrinaire in their liberalism—beginning with supreme faith in an elected legislature, and showing at the same time an undue distrust of the executive, because the execu- tive power was still lodged with the King—the French Revolution led quickly to a rule by committees, to a government that was almost entirely executive in its concentration of power; as though the initial error had to find its compensation in a flight to the opposite extreme. At first it was freedom that was the battle- cry, and the rights of men were to be guarded even against the state; but the very fervour and exhilaration that this engendered, enabled the Revolution to move upon its own momentum to an inversion of its original

ideals. Very soon those who dissented from a predominant party, even those who only tried to mod-
erate its frenzy, were being treated as second-class
citizens. Such people were enemies of the Revolution;
they were traitors to the state.

Within four years the transition had been made.
France passed from the liberalism of 1789 to the bru-
talities and hysterias of a dictatorship—a dictatorship
more formidable because it rested on the "insurrection," the menace of the inspired mob, the People
working by direct action. And when the enemies of
France—Englishmen in particular—cried out in the
next thirty years their abhorrence of the French Revolution, what they abhorred was not the liberalism of
1789 but the thing they called Jacobinism—the
Jacobin dictatorship. This dictatorship—in the name
of the "general will" but irrespective of the question
whether it answered to anything more than the views
of a mere minority—not only attempted to discipline
or subdue France to an acceptance of its republican
ideals, but sought to change a whole civilization and
to reconstruct the very fabric of the state—sought to
create a new machinery, a new code of laws, even a
new calendar and a new religion; and, in a manner
scarcely conceivable hitherto, mobilised the resources
of France for war.

Whether the French Revolution led the world to
democracy is a question which has still to be decided.
There can be no doubt of one of its effects: it led to
the development of a more powerful type of state. It
produced a state more calculated for efficiency, more
highly-organized, more wide in its competence, more
terrifying in its power than any which then existed;
and it made government more irresistible from the

fact that henceforward government was to claim to be the incontrovertible agent of the new god, the organic people. It is in this sense most of all that Napoleon is the heir—if he is not the logical conclusion—of the French Revolution. Before his time the real inversion of ideals had taken place—France had seen Jacobinism, dictatorship, totalitarianism, the Reign of Terror. Before his time the new engine, the high-powered state, had come into the hands of a minority, had even been abused for private purposes. And even before he came one may say that he was half-expected. If there had been no Napoleon there would still have had to be a coup d'état, as we shall see. By a process which has been repeated many times since—always with similar technique and similar tricks of intellectual sleight-of-hand—the Revolution itself found formulas for the future enslavement of mankind, and produced, while Napoleon was still unknown, all the ingredients of his system—the dictatorship based on the plebiscite.

In a parallel manner the French revolutionary war passed—again, so to speak on its own momentum, by a process of natural adaptation to each problem as it arose—towards the inversion of its original ideals, until a war for freedom and self-determination had changed into a fabulous career of conquest. Besides creating the modern state the French Revolution became the mother of modern war; for when all men become conscious that they are partners in public policy patriotism itself acquires a new exhilaration; the age of deified Peoples supervenes; the conditions exist for the intensification of modern nationalism. The French Revolution puts an end to the gentlemanly warfare—almost the mimic warfare we might be tempted to say—of the eighteenth-century professional armies. It puts an end to the urbane diplomatic game played with counters by cosmopolitan aristocrats, cynical sometimes, yet too worldly-wise for the last insanities of unforgiving passion. It brings conscription, the nation in arms, the mobilisation of all the resources of the state for unrelenting conflict. It heralds the age when peoples, woefully ignorant of one another, bitterly uncomprehending, lie in uneasy juxtaposition watching one another's sins with hysteria and indignation. It heralds Armageddon, the giant conflict for justice and right between angered populations each of which thinks it is the righteous one. So a new kind of warfare is born—the modern counterpart to the old conflicts of religions.

Napoleon had a great advantage. The new type of polity, the new kind of warfare, a national army, and the exaltation of an awakened people were ready beforehand. The machinery that was there for him to develop and use put him a century in advance of his European enemies. He had to fight only *anciens régimes* of various kinds, systems in which the idea of the state had as yet been only imperfectly realized; decrepit empires, loosely-knit oligarchies, benevolent despotisms, discontented peoples—states which we should say were not yet rationalised, still encumbered with the fossilisations of former ages. And Napoleon's enemies, even if they could, were unwilling to imitate his system—unwilling to call their peoples into partnerships with them even for the purpose of defeating their great enemy; for they knew that this itself would be something in the nature of a surrender to Jacobinism; they knew that they would only be unleashing a monster that was to be dangerous ultimately to themselves.

So, to lessen the wonder of Napoleon, we must say that it was the French Revolution that generated power. And the French Revolution threw upon the world ideas and principles which have been actualised since in so far as they have served the cause of power. To lessen what we may consider to be the crime of Napoleon we may add that dictatorship of some sort lay in the dialectic of events themselves. Liberty comes to the world from English traditions, not from French theories; and the French Revolution contains within itself the complete pattern of the inverse process—the process from an initial liberalism to a higher distillation of tyranny. When reminded once of what he owed to Rousseau, Napoleon replied that the world might some day learn to wish that both Rousseau and he had never been born. His opportunity was great, but if we may be permitted for a moment to think of his career in the terms that he was always so ready to use, we may say that it can have been nothing less than Destiny itself which created for such an opportunity such a man.

Chapter 2

The Rise of Bonaparte

HE WAS born in Corsica on August 15, 1769, when France was completing the subjection of that island. He was the son of Charles Marie de Bonaparte, a scheming attorney, who was lively but lacked firmness and fibre; and of Letizia, an admirable, hard-headed woman, who governed a large unruly family with spartan energy and virtue. He was educated in France where we find him curiously thrown in upon himself, solitary, intense, and made to feel a foreigner; and being frugal and excessively industrious he was not without his angularities—unwilling to give his mind to those adjustments which seem to be indispensable for social success. His homesickness, his attempt to take charge of the family after the premature death of his father, his willingness almost to starve for the sake of his brothers, show the strength of that feeling for family which was so remarkable throughout his career. He was rich in his instinctive life, and over-ready to misuse it; over-quick, for example, in his youth to plunge into the sentimentalities of Rousseau. On this side he never learned how to educate himself, remaining curiously banal in his emotional structure; and he was liable at any time to be filled with melancholy by the sound of a village church-bell. We must not imagine him as merely a clever man; even as a child he was masterful and seemed to radiate power. He is a giant like Beethoven—his genius rising from colossal emotional pressures, residing one may say in all the fibres of his personality. We must see him even as a youth living under this psychological pressure, even contemplating suicide—one of those intense terrible burning minds that for a time seem to eat themselves away.

Above all he was a fiery Corsican, resentful of the dominion that France had acquired in his island. While training to be an artillery officer in France, he seemed to be setting his mind upon a political career at home. He read the history of various countries, wrote notes on Plato's *Republic,* studied the eighteenth-century *philosophes.* He became a disciple of Rousseau and wrote political treatises of a juvenile doctrinaire kind. Later he became the grand enemy of the doctrinaires, and especially of Rousseau; and with Metternich he imputed the disasters of his age to the currency of too facile generalisations in political science. He had shown himself a remarkable mathematician, though he was always careless and incompetent when faced with a simple addition sum. And history and mathematics—which contributed so much to the structure of his profounder mind—became the studies that he chiefly recommended, especially for those who were to govern states. In his youth, however, Corsica was his ambition, and Rousseau, who had praised the Corsicans, was his teacher. The opening of the French Revolution found him at Auxonne, still very poor, still a resentful patriot, and bitterly anti-French. He not only supported the Revolution but spent many months agitating and organising on its behalf in his home-country. The first political coup that he attempted was in Corsica, and, though he struggled desperately against great odds, he was eventually forced to admit defeat. It is only then that he throws himself into a military career, and, an exile from his own country, begins to court fortune inside France itself.

In the latter part of the eighteenth century a great change had been taking place in the teaching of the art of war. A new system of offensive warfare was being inculcated, and its methods were rapid and vigorous, unlike the cumbrous motions that armies had in earlier days. Attention was being paid to the swift concentration of force at a given point, to continuous energy in attack and pursuit, and continuous resourcefulness in whatever things would make for elasticity and surprise; the enemy was to have no breathing-space, and instead of being burdened with magazines and administrative *impedimenta* that so gravely conditioned the movements of older armies, the new army was to live on the country that was the scene of war—was even (as one writer said) to make war pay for itself. Technical developments and the advance of science had assisted this change in the theory of war—better roads, better maps, more mobile artillery, for example, permitted greater swiftness and elasticity, permitted greater skill in the timing and co-ordination of the complex movements of armies that operated in sections. And whereas artillery had once been cumbrous and its use had been static— making it more fitting for a siege, we might say, than for a campaign—Gribeauval had studied to render it more mobile, and to make more effective use of it in combination with the movements of the infantry. One writer, Guibert, had even foreseen the tremendous advantage that a country could have by surprising its enemies with this new kind of warfare. He had seen the further power that would come if the army were a citizen-army, and he is almost the prophet of the French Revolutionary Wars. He is the prophet even of Napoleon, for in one passage he shows the possibilities and the potentialities of a dictatorship.

Now it has been shown that Bonaparte learned his science as a commander not merely from military history, for which genuine materials were not always at hand; and not merely from experience, as one might expect—some of his principles clearly appear in the first military plans that he produced—but he learned from Gribeauval, from Guibert, and from Bourcet's *Guerre de Montagnes*; and he was the favourite pupil of Du Theil, one of the chief exponents of the new teaching. Bonaparte plunges into the new methods from the start, and his writings contain passages directly reminiscent of the authors who had preached them. What has been called the general physiognomy of a battle, as we should infer it from these teachers of the art of war, is the physiognomy of a Napoleonic battle, unlike the fighting of an earlier age. It has been shown that Bonaparte learned warfare in the first place by learning principles, and not by mysterious intuition; though, far from following the manner of mediocre men who learn principles by rote, he showed his genius by his way of powerfully apprehending them. He seized upon the principles that were elemental and directed them to the complex and moving problems that a strategist has to face; doing this with versatility and precision, and with masterly control of the super-abundant details. Many of his principles of war have been traced back to eighteenth-century teachers of military science; but one can be sure that a mere verbal knowledge of principles will never transform a man into a great commander. It

will not alter the nature of a military officer merely
to learn from a book that a soldier should have elasticity and a rare copiousness of mind. So, though it
was Bourcet, for example, who taught that a military
plan should be mobile and multiple in character—
admitting of alternative courses of action in response
to whichever of the various possible moves the enemy
might make—it was Bonaparte who, as a strategist
in politics and war, had a mind so to speak congested
with alternatives, and possessed the elasticity that
enabled him to suspend the final choice and withhold
his decision until events should have given him his
cue.

He was fortunately away from Paris during the
early part of the Reign of Terror, but he was intimate
with Robespierre's brother and when the Robespierres
were guillotined in July 1794 he himself was in
danger, and even spent a short time in prison. He
was desirous of a strong government and a vigorous
prosecution of the foreign war, however; and he supported the conservative movement which sought to
place the government further away from the caprice
of the populace. In 1795 he saved the new regime in
Paris by firing on the mob which for so long had controlled or diverted the course of the Revolution. We
may note that it was really from this moment that he
became a celebrity in the capital. Then he married
the Creole, Josephine de Beauharnais, a widow some
years older than he—a woman who for a time seems
to have greatly under-estimated him. Her connections
with the rulers of France may have done something
to facilitate her husband's rise. He had been general
in command of the artillery of the army of Italy, had
learned much during this experience and had made

repeated projects for the conduct of the Italian war. It is clear that all the time he had been impressing himself upon his colleagues and his government; and in February 1796 he was given supreme command in Italy. Then began the campaign which was to bring Piedmont to heel and drive the Austrians out of their province of Lombardy—the campaign which was to make Napoleon the idol of France within a year.

Perhaps when we have studied this campaign we have seen it as too heroic an enterprise, charged too heavily with the force of his genius. Certainly a great opportunity was at hand, and fortune was very favourable to him. Already the coalition was breaking up, and when he began by separating the Piedmontese from the Austrian troops—when he succeeded in eliminating Piedmont from the war, by the conclusion of an armistice strategically very favourable to himself —he may have appeared to be a worker of wonders, but the Piedmontese, divided in counsels, were a half-hearted enemy already. Already they were suspected of desiring to escape from the war and it would be wrong to imagine that they had been reduced by a sublime military victory. Bonaparte put the Austrians at a disadvantage in the next stage of the war by in-fringing the neutrality of the Duke of Parma in his crossing of the Po; the Austrians had prepared to re-sist him at this river but they had laudably failed to anticipate of forestall the ruse that he adopted. It did not take much—an army of something like 40,000 men, moving rapidly and operating at times almost as a raiding force—to induce the smaller states of Italy to submit to the exactions of the French commander; and in accordance with the orders of his government Bonaparte despatched booty—money and works of art—to the French capital. On repeated occasions the Austrians gave him the advantage by dividing the forces that they sent to Italy to meet him.

The campaign produced great displacements in Italy and seems to gain in magnitude as a result; but a remarkable circumstance that contributed to its importance is independent of Napoleon Bonaparte himself. Italy did not merely remain a corpse while the Austrians and the French carried on their warfare in the north. A historic order, itself hollow and full of shams, failed to maintain itself when the impact came. An *ancien régime* that could continue in an eighteenth-century world of diplomatic etiquette and could flourish on the political indifference of the masses, now felt the contact of modern gangster politics, and quivered at the touch. In Italy there was something like an earthquake, shaking the feet of Bonaparte as well as of the older dynasties and though the Directors had ordered Bonaparte not to encourage revolutionary movements, though they only wanted to occupy an Austrian province in North Italy in order to force the court of Vienna to accept their terms in Germany, though they were anxious to be quickly rid of any commitments in Italy, Bonaparte disobeyed them, for he felt his own position to be in danger from the shifting sands around him—from the revolutionary movements that were taking place. He took these movements under his patronage so that he could have them under his control.

Furthermore, having induced his government to extend its original plan and allow an invasion of Austria, he pushed his troops northwards into enemy country until he came to be in danger from his own incautious advance. He then broke his instructions once more and persuaded the Austrians to conclude preliminaries of peace before they realised the weakness of his position. And the very terms of the agreement that he concluded contravened the whole policy of his government at home. He secured Belgium for France but he failed to achieve what the Directors wanted—the left bank of the Rhine; instead of this he induced the Austrians to surrender the Milanese and to take in exchange—what they themselves had been desiring—the rich lands of Venice, which had hitherto been a neutral state. So while appearing to dictate peace as he menaced the capital of Austria, he really made a composition very favourable to the enemy; at the same time he increased the commitments of the French government in Italy and destroyed any hope of a speedy return to normality in the peninsula.

He had become so popular in France that the government could not afford to come into conflict with him. He had furthermore made the army his political party, for he knew how to inspire his troops and he had changed the face of fortune for them. His masterly moves, his heroic feats, his infectious spirit, his stirring bulletins had given the soldiers supreme confidence in their leader. So he was able to change the original purpose of the campaign, and to turn the Italian war into an end in itself instead of a mere diversion against the Austrian left wing. He was able to negotiate the definitive treaty of Campo-Formio in 1797 and by hectoring diplomacy he forced the Austrians to accept a revision of the preliminary agreement. The Habsburgs now gave virtual consent to the acquisition of the left bank of the Rhine by the French Republic; they themselves acquired Venice and the Illyrian coast. The establishment of republics in the rest of North Italy enabled Bonaparte to assist in the making of new constitutions in these states—sham constitutions, however, working under the shadow of his military power, mock republics in which he himself appointed the officials and controlled the government.

So Bonaparte, making virtue sometimes of necessity —but doing it with imagination and supreme audacity —enlarged his rôle and became commander, diplomat, constitution-maker, arbiter of Italy, until one might feel that now the army was running away with the state. We shall not be surprised, therefore, to discover that by this time the army had assumed an important political rôle even in the internal affairs of France. The five Directors who were at the head of the executive government in France were not only in disagreement with one another but in conflict with the two legislative bodies. In spite of their attempts to control the results of the elections that were held in March and April 1797, the voting resulted in the victory of a combination of what where called the "royalists" and the "constitutional royalists." The old laws against reactionaries and exiles and refractory priests were now being repealed by the legislature, in defiance of the executive; and the Directors representing the vested interests of the Revolution, the new rich, the bourgeoisie, saw the danger to the regime. They did not feel strong enough to engineer what we should call a political coup d'état and they did not dare to appeal, as in the great days of the Revolution, to the direct action of the Paris mob. They determined to resort to the military. An initial attempt, however, in which General Hoche was to have assisted them, was forestalled by the legislature.

It happened that the opposition attacked Bonaparte

in their press, and he retorted with angry denunciations of a royalist plot. Political propaganda began to issue from the army, coming in the name of the soldiers, who were the real patriots now. Bonaparte offered to send the leading Directors three million pounds for the carrying out of a coup d'état. He despatched General Augereau to Paris to serve the anti-royalist party, and Augereau, who was ready to bully and brag, was only too anxious to adopt a political rôle. With the army behind them, with many precautionary movements of troops, and with Augereau in command in Paris, the majority of the Directors carried out the coup d'état of Fructidor (September 1797), having severed the communications between Paris and the provinces until they could assure themselves of success. It was a conservative coup d'état, intended to save the regime; but it comprised a military encirclement of the Legislative Councils and a drastic annulment of recent elections. It implied the dismissal of two of the Directors, both of whom were to have been deported, though one took refuge in flight. It was followed by summary executions, and penal legislation against the defeated party. Bonaparte, by sending Augereau, had covered himself in case the coup d'état should prove a failure; but very soon he was claiming the result as a victory for his own army, a victory of the patriots over the politicians. The army was now definitely introduced into politics and could, with pardonable self-righteousness, feel itself the arbiter in the state. For Bonaparte, indeed, the whole episode may be regarded as a stage on the road to power.

After his return from Italy, Bonaparte for a moment entertained the idea of an invasion of England, but came to the conclusion that it was an unpromising enterprise for a power that lacked the command of the sea—impossible unless one could make a surprise crossing. By this time his mind had become occupied with wild dreams of conquest in the east, for even while he had been in Italy he had begun to say that the Mediterranean must be a French sea, that Malta and the Ionian Isles were essential to France, that the Turkish empire was ripe for overthrow. Talleyrand, the French minister for foreign affairs, had already discerned that Bonaparte would make history, and had seen the policy of establishing confidential relations with him; he helped to make Bonaparte's eastern design more practicable, to established it in its historical context, and to persuade the government to support it. In the reign of Louis XVI projects of an enterprise in Egypt had already been put before the French government. In the period when France was nursing the idea of "revanche" after England's colonial victories in the Seven Years' War this had been considered as a possible threat to our Indian empire. It had been discussed again in the period of the revolutionary wars and now there was an idea of landing an expedition in Egypt before the British government should have any suspicion of its destination. The Directory had been anxious not to lose the traditional friendship of the Sultan, who had suzerainty over Egypt. The expedient was adopted of attacking the province in the name of the Sultan himself, and pretending to deliver it from the Mamelukes and the menace of the English. In May 1798 Bonaparte set out with instructions to capture Malta and "drive the English out of all their possessions in the East"; to secure for France the exclusive possession of the Red Sea and to revive the fortunes of Egypt, preventing if possible any offence to the Sultan of Turkey. He captured Malta and found rich booty there in June; and then, eluding the British fleet, he landed near Alexandria.

As an operation directed against England the enterprise was singularly unsuccessful. Bonaparte's attack on Malta only led to our acquisition of that island. The threat to India only quickened us to a greater effort there, and this resulted in the defeat and death of Tippoo Sahib who had hoped for French assistance. The threat in the Mediterranean only led to the naval battle of Aboukir, which left Nelson supreme in that sea and cut Bonaparte's communications with France. As part of the Napoleonic epic, however, the expedition was not without its grandeur —its romantic episodes, its constructive feats, its picturesque victories, its tales of endurance in the desert. It is the beginning of the modern history of Egypt; the project of a Suez Canal has its antecedents in this period. It was Bonaparte's surveyors on the isthmus of Suez who produced the startling view that the Red Sea and the Mediterranean had different levels. Remarkable ingenuity was used to make the French army independent—as it now had to be—of supplies from France. A government was organised, with the ostensible participation of native councils, and the taxes and the agriculture of Egypt were taken in hand. Bonaparte conferred with the religious teachers of Islam (whom he treated with great sympathy and skill) and conducted an extensive foreign policy with the whole Mohammedan world. As in Italy he learned the arts of a dictator in a foreign land, a conquered territory, before he came to the government of France. He had brought noted scientists with him and founded a scientific institute at Cairo, taking part himself for a time in the activities of this body. The course of the Nile was examined by engineers; Egypt was opened up to archaeological research; under the direction of Monge that great work, the *Description de l'Egypte,* was commenced. When the Turks declared war, Bonaparte marched to Syria to meet them, and he who had talked of the conquest of India now dreamed of capturing Constantinople and taking Europe "in the rear." He was held up at the siege of Acre where, over-dramatising himself, he later said that he missed his destiny. After a tragic return to Egypt—one so beset by suffering that it has been described as a foretaste of the retreat from Moscow in 1812—he came to Aboukir and defeated another army of Turks, which in the meantime had been sent to Egypt by sea. Then in August 1799, he left his army and set sail for France with a few companions—knowing that France had need of him at this moment, but not knowing that the Directory in its distress had actually sent him his recall.

His wife Josephine had given him anxiety during the Italian expedition. To his ardent and desperate love-letters she had replied, he said, as though she were a woman of fifty. In Egypt he obtained proof of her infidelity: and the whole experience in the mind of so earnest a lover, produced a distress which a biographer must not fail to note. He thought of divorce: he wrote to his brother:

> The veil is completely torn away . . . I am weary of human nature, and grandeur is only a burden to me. Feeling has withered; glory has become stale; at 29 I have drunk life to the dregs. There is nothing left for me now but to become a complete egoist.

Of the army that had been sent to Egypt, not more than half ever returned to France. The Revolution could squander its man-power on a wild adventure, and Bonaparte like some blind force in nature never heeded the toll that he took in human lives. But in personal relations he could still have an almost feminine gentleness. And when on his return to France his step-children interceded for Josephine, he took her back into his affections; for he could not resist their tears.

Because the fires burned in him more intensely than in other people, the conduct of Josephine had a deep effect, leaving him without the gift or even the desire for intimacy in human relations. More and more he seemed to emerge as a man possessed, a man under a curse—"I am a fragment of rock launched into space," he said. It would seem that the higher he rose, the harder he worked—he would give himself only eight minutes for lunch and twelve minutes for dinner—and if he was making a formal entry into a city he would abstract himself, he would be elaborating, for example, a plan of maritime operations that would be written down when the ceremony was over. "I am always working," he said, "even when I am at dinner or at the theatre and in the middle of the night." This capacity for work was a nervous complaint, almost we might say the equivalent of St. Vitus's dance; as though he would be unhappy if he stopped to contemplate, as though the wheels must keep revolving or great pressures would drive the man mad. We may feel at times that if he could have taken a holiday, if only he could have said, "Now we will relax and enjoy the fruits of all our striving," he might have been saved. But the tension would not relax; it was as though the springs inside him had been too tightly coiled. "My master has no bowels," he once remarked, "my master is the constitution of things." So upon executive details as well as upon the fine sweep of an imaginative exploit, he was able to turn the fierce light of his genius. All his intentness could be focussed upon technical points and he could see anomalies in complex pages of statistics. "If there is nobody to make gunpowder, I know how to manufacture it," he said; "gunwaggons—I know how to build them; if cannon are to be cast, I will cast them; if anybody needs to be taught the details of manœuvres, I will do the teaching." Even as an Emperor he would know when he was being cheated in the price of shoes for his army, when a regiment was buying too many shoes, and when the harness supplied for the horses was badly made. To that strange purposeless conformation of the brain which produces now the human calculating-machine, now the infant-prodigy and now the champion chess-player, he added the faculty that superintends, the force that makes these gifts purposeful and mighty—a genuine power of intellect. Restless, possessed, without the aptitude for leisure, but driven by his genius—that "genius" which makes its local depredations even when it falls only in a casual way on a suburban poet—Bonaparte was now to find a magnificent projection for his energies, to capture for himself all the resources and the unsuspected power of the first of modern states.

Chapter 3

First Consul

IN 1799 the ports of France were decayed, the roads in disrepair and infested with brigands. Public buildings everywhere—prisons, barracks, schools, for example—had been allowed to fall into a state of neglect. Parisian society had an appearance of disintegration—the new rich, in their glory, apparently heedless of the public good; the masses politically indifferent, content to leave government to the professionals; divorces and scandals innumerable and constant rumour of corruption in high places; and everybody weary of continued war, weary of the drain upon manpower, money, and horses—ten years of revolution and conflict, of taut nerves and exhausting indignations, having brought the world by inevitable reaction to a condition of nausea and disillusionment. A second coalition had been organised against France; besides Russia, Austria and England, it included Naples, Portugal and Turkey. The French had been almost driven out of Italy and were being pressed on the side of the Rhine. The situation was one in which Frenchmen in particular are ready to cry out for a saviour.

It was a situation which also presented serious technical difficulties. Almost insuperable obstacles were placed upon a revision of the constitution. Three times —and these at three-year intervals—a revision had to be approved by the two houses of the legislature before the assembly that had power of amendment could even be brought into existence. The Directory had only held its power by virtue of what had been a succession of coups d'état; and a whole series of legislative measures (including such as took away the right to vote from men who were qualified by the constitution) had had the effect of infringing the fundamental law and abridging the liberties of citizens. Those who most wanted to preserve the regime and to confirm the achievements of the Revolution became the most anxious for constitutional change; at the same time they were ready to admit that this must imply another coup d'état. For two years—ever since the events of Fructidor—some of the Directors had been meditating such a move; they were resentful of their weakness against the legislature, and, also, they had their vested interests and their private schemes for power. It was being said now that the executive was the general will, that it was the legislature which was betraying the Revolution: Bonaparte, supporting the policy of revision, had been eager to insist upon this point. In proposing constitutions for the new republics that were emerging as client-states on the borders of France, the Directors were careful not entirely to duplicate the system of government that was working so imperfectly at home; and by the amendments that they tried to introduce they showed the nature of their desires.

By 1799 some of the Directors were thinking of making use of a popular general for a coup d'état that would increase their power. They fixed first of all upon General Joubert; but Joubert was killed before the scheme was mature. Among these Directors was Sieyès, a political geometrician—a kind of professional constitution-maker—the man who in 1789 had caused ferment by his pamphlet: *What is the Third Estate?* It is curious that one who did so much to bring about the

Revolution should have had so great a part in the conspiracy that put an end to it. Indeed he was distrustful of Bonaparte at first, and some diplomacy was needed before the two men were brought together. Sieyès was soon to learn that he had acquired not a tool, not even an ally, but a master.

It was on October 9, 1799, that Bonaparte, having eluded the English fleet in the Mediterranean, made his dramatic return from Egypt and reached the shores of France with a handful of friends. Though the worst moment in the foreign war had passed he was greeted as a legendary hero, a heaven-sent deliverer; and in regard to the coup d'état that was obviously in the air he was told that he would find the work already three-quarters done for him. He was able, therefore, to adopt a broader basis for his enterprise, and conceive of something grander than a mere military coup or party victory; something that should gather into itself the great tide of popular expectation and enthusiasm of which Franch was the witness at this moment.

The technique of the coup d'état rested on the complicity of ministers and Directors. It was facilitated by the fact that the old government could be induced to destroy itself from within. The intrigue was carried out by politicians in their studies—"in the lobbies of the two Assemblies . . . everywhere in fact save in the offices of the General Staff." Bonaparte showed even that he feared danger from the army—from republican fervour there, or from the jealousy of possible rivals amongst the officers. He even showed himself more unwilling than Sieyès to begin with a resort to violent measures—counted indeed on over-reaching Sieyès precisely by putting himself above parties and emerging as the representative of France. If he secured the ovations of the troops as well as the cheers of the citizens at this time, that was because he had convinced soldiers and civilians alike that he was determined to establish liberty and save the republic.

On November 9 (the 18th Brumaire) the Council of Ancients, which we might describe as the equivalent of the Senate, decreed the removal of the whole legislature to St. Cloud on the pretext of the danger from an alleged Jacobin plot. Such a decree was within the competence of that Council and once it had been issued the other partner in the legislature, the Council of Five Hundred, was compelled to adjourn without further discussion. Paris, which had imposed itself so often on the Revolution, could no longer intervene—the legislature was to be out of its reach. The Council of Ancients, acting this time in a matter outside its competence, but on the pretext of the alleged emergency, then gave Bonaparte command of all troops near Paris, including those which guarded the legislature. Two Directors, Sieyès and his ally Roger-Ducos, who were in the conspiracy, now resigned; and their colleague Barras was made to see the advantage of resigning too, instead of attempting any resistance. As a majority of the five Directors was needed to give validity to executive action, these three resignations had the effect of leaving France without an executive. The two legislative bodies were to be confronted with this situation on the following day, the 19th Brumaire; and they were to be induced to suspend their own sessions, to commit the government to three consuls, Bonaparte, Sieyès and Roger-Ducos, and to confide to these consuls the task of creating a new constitution for the republic.

The delay proved almost fatal to the plot; for enemies had time to take alarm. No evidence existed for the alleged "anarchist" conspiracy that had been the pretext for all the emergency measures. When Bonaparte entered the Council of Five Hundred on the 19th there were cries of "Down with Dictators" and he was roughly handled. It was his brother Lucien, the President of that Council, who saved the day by giving the summons to the troops who were waiting outside. He said that deputies in the pay of England were maltreating the patriots and must be driven out of the chamber. He declared that he would kill Napoleon himself, if Napoleon ever betrayed the cause of liberty. The soldiers then rushed to disperse the deputies, crying, "Long live Bonaparte. Down with the Lawyers." In a manner much less regular than had been arranged, a chosen number of the deputies of both houses met later in the day to appoint the three consuls with the required powers.

Bonaparte's ascendancy not merely in the army but in the country made it unnecessary for him to act henceforward as the tool of the politicians. He might allow Sieyès to design the shell of the new constitution, but he took care to absorb the real virtue of it into himself. While Sieyès, for example, put the executive into the hands of three consuls—intending the First Consul to be nothing more than a figure-head—Bonaparte accepted the diagram but reduced it to nullity by securing that he himself should engross all the power.

He had out-manœuvred the intriguers themselves. He was made First Consul and head of the executive for ten years. He clinched the matter with all the formalities of a plebiscite, and though we need not be deceived by this we must not assume that he was un-

acceptable to France. He now announced that the
Revolution was completed, that the era of proscriptions
and coups d'état had come to an end. He affected to
proclaim that parties and civil strife were to be forgotten and that he had been called to bring reconciliation and the healing of wounds. He saw what was to be
gained at this moment by imagination and synthesis
—realised the capital he could make by combining the
achievements of the Revolution and the virtues of the
ancien régime. He invited the *émigrés* back to France
and men who had proscribed one another, regicides
and aristocrats, Catholics and unbelievers, were persuaded to work together, persuaded to cooperate in
the building of a unified nation at last. At this period
he was wise in his choice of subordinates, and, looking
for ability irrespective of high birth and former political creeds, he collected in the service of France a
greater assemblage of talent, working in a closer col-
laboration, than had perhaps ever been known before;
while he himself, more capable of unremitting work
than any of the rest—moving from one topic to another with a mind always instantly in focus and in a
state of high compression—would range through the
various activities of government, giving his stamp to
all, and revivifying all.

This was the time when France achieved that organ-
ization which the Revolution had been attempting to
establish—achieved a structure which in essentials has
persisted through all intervening regimes down to the
present-day. What endured of the French Revolution
was that which was ratified and riveted by Bonaparte.
What spread throughout Europe—influencing Italy
for example—were the things that he and his armies
carried. Amongst these things we must not look for

liberty, for, in spite of the optical illusions of history, the development of freedom lies elsewhere, far from the hysterias and cataclysms of this violent age. The real history of freedom is the profounder story of the slow growth of reasonableness among men.

On his advent to power Bonaparte promised peace. The country was vociferous for that. He regarded it as the initial mandate that France had given him, and all his language signified that here was his mission. He knew at the same time that the French would not be satisfied with peace at any price. He knew that this meant, paradoxically, for the time being, the continuance of the war. The French were to be reconciled in the meantime by the thought that at any rate now they were fighting to some purpose. By one treaty after another—treaties not merely tolerable but glorious—Bonaparte eventually carried out the mandate which he regarded as having been entrusted to him. The Peace of the Consulate that he achieved is an imposing thing, wide and magnificent like the Pax Romana. It cannot be denied that in the first place Napoleon built his power on great and systematic services to France.

It was all the more remarkable in that the success which he gained was achieved with a minimum of actual warfare. In June 1800, after crossing the Great St. Bernard with his army, he won the battle of Marengo and broke the power of the Austrians in Lombardy. As his position in France had been precarious and intrigues were being renewed even now during his absence from Paris, the battle was of capital importance: Marengo consolidated his power and dismayed his enemies at home. Austria, defeated again by Moreau at Hohenlinden in December, concluded the Treaty of Lunéville in February 1801; and as this treaty virtually repeated the arrangements made at Campo-Formio, it had the effect of confirming to France the acquisitions of the Revolution. Bonaparte cleverly flattered the Czar Paul, and lured him not only out of the hostile coalition but into a series of measures that were unfriendly to England. Disputes with Naples and the United States were settled by treaty; and peace was made with the Ottoman Turk. Finally at Amiens in 1802 there was signed the definitive treaty of peace with England—the terms being so favourable to France that it is not easy to see why the British government gave its consent to the arrangement. This crowned and completed the Peace of the Consulate and Bonaparte was rewarded with the consulship for life.

Remarkable in another respect is the manner in which Bonaparte put an end to the conflict with the Church. It had seemed that the Revolution had found an issue that was fundamental when it came to a cleavage with Roman Catholicism. If reconciliation and at least a *modus vivendi* were established, for this achievement Bonaparte himself must have the credit. When he died twenty years later one man shed tears for him, and this was Pius VII, a Pope whom he had greatly misused. When asked the reason for his tears Pius replied that it had required great courage in Bonaparte to restore the Catholic religion. Bonaparte had a profound insight into the importance of religion for the mass of the people. He had real historic sense and, as one may see from his propaganda, a knowledge of the hidden half-instinctive things that have to be catered for in irrational human beings. The men around him, however, the men whose intrigues were his chief danger, and even his own agents, were bitterly hostile to his policy. Yet he preserved the revolutionary organ- ization of the Church; he preserved the system by which Church lands had been expropriated and the clergy became paid servants of the state; he preserved, what for centuries had existed in France, the state con- trol of ecclesiastical patronage. And in return he did not make Catholicism the state religion, but only ac- knowledged it as the predominant one in France. After this agreement, this *Concordat,* with the Papacy had been made, he put forward some Organic Articles which were issued unilaterally, not by any agreement but as a mere fiat of the state. They gave the govern- ment powers of police in matters of religion and were bound to provoke immediate resentment on the part of the Pope.

His great instrument of government was a Council of State, which he inherited from the Revolution. It was through this that he carried out his re-organiza- tion of France and it was here that he found real col- laboration in his early years when he was willing to learn from others. He enhanced its competence in order to weaken both legislative assemblies and minis- tries; and it was used not only for administrative but for some judicial purposes and had quasi-legislative power. He had ministers and some of these held office for long periods; but everything was done to prevent them from acquiring authority of their own. He dealt with each minister separately and did not allow them to attain corporate strength by meeting as a cabinet. They were not Secretaries of State like ministers of the *ancien régime;* there was a separate Secretary who served for all, countersigning and authenticating the decisions that they made. There was no chief minister, however, and for a time though ministers might be consulted they could not vote in the Council of State. Furthermore they were weakened by the duplication of offices—besides the minister of finance, there was a minister of the Public Treasury, for example; and within the various departments there would be administrative committees, manned by members of the Council of State and almost independent of the minister concerned, the general directorate of Public Instruction being only one of many instances of this.

Local self-government was virtually abolished and the departments of France were ruled by prefects nominated in Paris. These were assisted by councils similarly appointed, while the mayors of all towns of any considerable size were also the nominees and agents of the central government. Able prefects carried the Bonapartist administration into every region of the country; and the work of the Revolution in demolishing the ancient parlements, the privileged corporations, the guilds, and the great crop of local rights that had abridged the sovereignty of French kings, enabled the new administration to control the country without obstruction.

It was not until 1802 that the real effects of the regime became evident. From March 1802 to April 1803 France was at peace with all the world; the Consulate was in its glory; and the whole country seemed transformed. It is apparent that Bonaparte regarded it as his function to discipline society after years of disturbance and anarchy; and it was this policy—so congenial to the spirit of an autocracy—that gave his reforms their character. Brigandage ceased. Public works were undertaken. Educational reform—which the Revolution had left imperfect—was developed with the view of producing good soldiers and citizens. In the *lycées* that were opened during the Consulate every quarter of an hour in the day was regulated by the government time-table; the libraries of 3,000 books were everywhere the same in accordance with a list that had been drawn up in Paris; the study of the natural sciences and of what we should call technology were of great importance; every movement of classes was signalised by the beating of drums and carried out in military fashion; and boys above the age of twelve were trained in the use of arms.

There was one task—the unification of local systems of law, and the creation of a legal code—which had long been meditated under the monarchs of the old regime and had been attempted by the Revolution; but the energy of Bonaparte was needed to drive the project to completion. The work was put into the hands of eminent jurists with a Breton to represent the Customary Law that was current in one part of France, and two southerners to speak for the Roman Law that prevailed in another part; and the fact that technical lawyers were employed instead of parliamentary legislators, the fact also that no revolutionary jurisconsult was put on the commission, though there were such at Bonaparte's disposal, indicated a desire to keep in touch with history, and to "filter the legislation of the revolution so that it could be put into the framework of French traditional law."

The Code was examined before the Council of State, and it was here that Bonaparte chiefly collaborated in its production; for, though only just turned thirty, he presided at this Council over the ablest men of the day, all of them older than he and many of them twenty or thirty years older; and in the first series of discussions on the subject of the Civil Code—those which concerned the most important section, dealing with Persons—he attended the great majority of the sessions and after a short time took a leading part in the business. He would keep this Council sitting for hours at a stretch, and when the members seemed weary he would jog them into activity, patting them on the back and saying "Come, gentlemen, we must earn the money that France is paying us." If the topic did not interest him he would scribble automatically during the course of the meeting: "You are all brigands," or "Oh Lord how I love you," reproducing the same sentence over and over again. But we see him also in these early years anxious to learn, inquiring the definition of words—for even his knowledge of French was faulty—or asking how things were done under the governments that preceded his; and it is evident that he was skilful in cross-examining experts, knowing the strategic questions that would bring him quickly to the heart of a matter. He learned not so much by reading as by conversation, we are told. He did not attempt to hide his ignorance of points of administrative technique. Also, though he did not make all the decisions, his was often the energy that drove others to decide.

As regards the Civil Code it has been demonstrated that Bonaparte was not a theoretical partisan of the Roman system of law as was once believed. It has been shown also that he was not responsible for the restoration of the power of the father in the family, which was one of the features of the Code. When he spoke in favour of divorce and adoption he was not working with an eye upon his own future or upon the problems that his own family were to give him. And though his insistence upon the subjection of women

o their husbands may have been due in part to the
rivolity of Josephine, even here he seems to have had
n mind rather the general laxity of manners and
morals that had been displayed during the Revolution,
especially in Paris, a laxity for which he held the
women to have been in a special sense responsible.
n general it was he rather than the professional law-
ers who had learned something from the philosophic
writers of the eighteenth century. It was he who reminded the others that manners and morals had
altered, that the world had had "a change of heart,"
that the lawyers, for example, were still legislating
or the days when marriages had been arranged for
he respective parties by their relatives. Repeatedly
he declared that he intervened in the discussions as a
statesman, not as a lawyer—as one who had charge
of the general interest of the land and knew the kind
of society that he wished to organise but was too dis-
creet to quarrel with the technicians on their own
ground. Often it was he who saw the human issues
that were involved in a piece of legislation, telling
he lawyers for example, "There is something more
n marriage than a mere union of names and goods";
and declaring on one occasion that a play would be
hissed off the stage if its plot were worked out on the
principles that the lawyers were putting forward. He
wished to legislate at the expense of large owners of
property but in favour of the small possessors. It was
he who showed the desire to secure a system that
would encourage the growth of population in France.
On many matters he gave way to the lawyers and one
recent jurist has expressed the regret that in some of
these things he did give way—has shown also that in
some cases legislation since the Napoleonic era has

brought the code into closer conformity with Bonaparte's desires. The members of the Council of State
were impressed by his insight into even the technical
side of the legal problems; and we know that he meditated deeply on the Code, desiring to be not a military
dictator but a civilian ruler, a master of the arts of
peace. He hoped to make the law simple, but as he
said at St. Helena, the lawyers could not be prevented
from introducing complexity; and a remark that he
made after the achievement of the Code shows the
vigour of his lay mind in matters pertaining to the
law: "Oh, gentlemen, we have cleansed the Augean
stable. In the name of God let us not litter it up
again."

Finally the career of Bonaparte taught Louis-
Napoleon, his nephew (whom we know as Napoleon
III) and taught any other statesman who might aspire
to a dictatorship of a similar kind, that danger comes
from the intelligentsia, the middle classes, the ama-
teurs of politics, who are apt to be jealous and alert
when an autocracy is gathering power. From the
lower classes, on the other hand, great support and
wonderful loyalty can be evoked. These may be grateful to a leader who shows concern for the material
welfare of the people. And in lean and hungry times
political franchises may seem a jest and a superfluity
Bonaparte reformed the finances of the country and
put an end to much of the corruption of an earlier
day. He confirmed the peasants in the possession of
the lands which the Revolution had released to them
and he provided the feeling of stability, the assurance
that the possession of these lands was no longer a
precarious one. He was to become essentially the
peasants' Emperor, and the peasants were not sighing

for greater liberty now—not anxious for more political experiments. The work of the Consulate may be summarised in Bonaparte's formula: "We have finished with the romance of the Revolution, we must now begin its history. We must see what was real and politically possible in its principles, instead of grasping at their speculative and hypothetical side."

When he became First Consul he had just passed his thirtieth birthday, and had a lean and ascetic appearance. He was short in stature, however, and in succeeding years grew stouter, till he became the squat figure that is so familiar to us. All who came into direct contact with him seem to have been struck by his irresistible eyes. He could be so fascinating in personal interview that an old enemy like Blücher was later afraid to meet him lest he should come under his spell; but he had a nervous twitch that made men fear his displeasure, and some were frightened to find that even when the lower part of his face was smiling the eyes never seemed to smile. Also, in one of his mighty passions or in wilful caprice he might destroy any valuable object that lay at hand. He shaved himself, which few men did at that period—using a Birmingham razor, it is said; but unless he was reminded by his valet he might forget one side of his face. If, as sometimes happened, he had been so hurried with his eating that he made himself ill, then he was a pitiable figure; this hero of many battles would lean on Josephine and behave like a frightened child. Many who were close to him have left pictures of him, have shown how he was ungraceful on a horse, how he wasted his snuff, how he had no sense of the ridiculous; how when his mood was good, he would twist the ears of his valet till they hurt, or take down a volume of Corneille and declaim a passage; how, when he was glad he would sing with the tunelessness that comes from the very bottom of the universe, would bellow at a sentimental ditty or at "Marat, du peuple le vengeur," repeating the same words for a quarter of an hour because he could only remember the one line of words. Or he would amuse himself for a moment sealing the envelopes for his letters, until once he placed a letter to the Emperor of Austria in the letter addressed to the Czar. Lavish in some ways—and generous sometimes—he could be mean in little things, in slight economies in the palace for example; calculating the price that he was being charged per cup of coffee, and always saying: "When I was a sub-lieutenant things were not so dear." It was his firm view that he was always being cheated by tradesmen; and, while he would ask his valet, "Now, Monsieur Constant, what are you going to give me for the New Year," he himself would never buy a present for his servants; though he gained great devotion from those who were intimate with him, and he was remarkably generous in after-life to all who had had any connection with him in the hard days of his youth.

Chapter 4

The Progress of an Imperial Design

THE COLONIAL PROJECTS of the First Consul are like the first draft of an imperial design that proved abortive; and we may glance at them because they show with what fulness of meaning the word "opportunism" can be applied to his policy, and particularly to the diplomacy of the crucial years, which it will be necessary to examine for a moment. They show the versatility of a mind that had no closed plans for the future, with the railway-lines set out and the destination fixed—a mind prepared rather to make the most of all chances, pressing forward in every direction so long as doors remained open; eager indeed to run ahead of time and have schemes worked out for opportunities that might contingently arise. What we notice at this stage is elasticity: Bonaparte plays with systems and purposes, yet he can remain, so to speak, uncommitted. He is able without repining to cut his losses if a certain sector of the field becomes closed to him for any reason. Sometimes he seems to shoot in the dark, hoping that if he misses one thing he will hit another. He may calculate that in a certain eventuality a particular measure will be profitable in one way; but if the chances fall differently it will still be an advantage in another way, provided he gives a different turn to his purposes. Sometimes he makes an overture to see what will come of it, and it is not easy for the historian to say that he has any specific end in view. So he keeps the future fluid until events have closed in upon him and determined his path. Until 1806 at least, he does not know what course he will take at the next crossroads.

The overseas designs represented one of the possible lines of development for him at the moment. From Spain he gained Louisiana, providing compensation for the Bourbon family in Italy; and he alarmed the United States by his plans for the exploitation and military development of that colony. He sent Decaen to India with orders to discover the opportunities for French adventure there. He sent an expedition to reconquer San Domingo where the natives had risen in insurrection and thrown off their dependence on France. He patronized a mission to Australia, which, though nominally scientific, was perhaps not without side-reference to political possibilities. And he maintained his interest in Egypt, and even planned a punitive expedition that was to lead to the conquest of Algiers. It would appear that his schemes at this period envisaged and required the maintenance of peace, especially with England. And for the building up of his own marine service he had reason to avoid a further conflict for the time being. Perhaps it seemed natural to him that when he sent out his representatives—when even he gave his instructions to the commercial agents whom he was proposing to despatch to England—he should order them to transmit military information that would be useful in certain eventualities; but the knowledge of this—in the case of Egypt for example—only multiplied the apprehensions of his neighbours. Perhaps he did not desire war for the time being; but he behaved in a way that was bound to make peace impossible. And this was particularly true of his continental policy.

When Bonaparte acquired the direction of the government in France three regions of Europe were in a state that presented vast opportunities for change. They were regions in which the map of Europe was not yet fixed; where readjustments were expected and in fact had recently been taking place; where power was in some sense open to competition and the diplomatic tradition of the French monarchy not only forbade any indifference to the developments that might occur, but laid out the channels—set the initial pattern—that Bonaparte's diplomacy was to follow.

The first of these regions was the Italian peninsula, divided into small states but open to foreign domination. France, Spain and Austria had had the lordship there in turn, but never unchallenged, and it had been one of the subjects of the long Bourbon-Habsburg rivalry. Here Bonaparte had restored in the north that Cis-Alpine Republic, now the Italian Republic, which had been founded in 1797; and the leaders of that Republic had seen the wisdom, had recognised the necessity perhaps, of making him their President. Austria, however, had been compensated, as we have seen, with Venice and Illyria. She was still in a mood to challenge the extension of his power in the Italian peninsula.

A second region was Germany, divided at this time into hundreds of areas that claimed to be centres of sovereignty—ecclesiastical principalities, imperial towns, smaller and larger monarchies, and toy states that might have been invented for a comic opera—with frontiers often anomalous, crying out to be rationalised and rounded; and, over all, a Habsburg Emperor, standing as a symbol of antiquity and a source of dignities and honours. As imperial authority had dwindled almost to a shadow, Prussia and Austria were rivals for hegemony over the smaller states; and France could not be indifferent to the conflict— any enemy of the Habsburgs tended by tradition to be the protégé of France. Here, as in Italy, it was inevitable that Bonaparte should be on the side of territorial and constitutional change, and it had been in accordance with the constitution of things that Prussia should have long ago compromised with Revolutionary France. Here, again, therefore, the principal enemy was bound to be the conservative power of Austria.

The third region was the Ottoman empire in the conflict with which the Christian states had now for a century been the aggressors. Austria and Russia had been allies in the reconquest of this region, though reasons for mutual jealousy had already begun to emerge. In France a policy of diplomatic support and platonic patronage had created a traditional connection with the Turkish empire. Bonaparte now set out to continue this policy and he talked perpetually of maintaining the integrity of the Ottoman Porte. This formula would scarcely tie his hands if ever he himself should have the opportunity for an attack on that Empire. In the meantime it served as a warning to rivals, and tended to make him, since he chose to be the patron, at the same time the predominant influence in Constantinople.

One other region of Europe might be regarded as unstable in 1799, and this was Poland, the partition of which was very recent. Poland had been a client-state of France, and the connection between the two countries had deepened into one of sentiment. The partition of Poland had only been possible because France had been too weak at the strategic moments to prevent it. Sooner or later, therefore, we may expect Napoleon to remember that "France has never recognised the partition." He is ready to remind Prussia, Austria and Russia that the question of Poland is not yet closed.

From all this we can see how Napoleonic policy has its roots in the past, making use of customary responses to historic situations. It gathers into itself ancient sentiments, habitual animosities, old battle-cries—all the wealth of the diplomatic traditions of France. History gives the initial pattern of Napoleonic diplomacy, but what is new is the energy of the Revolution and the power of Napoleon himself—a power that leads him to transcend the original pattern, until he breaks it completely and it seems to disappear altogether. In all this we can see the value of Talleyrand, Bonaparte's foreign minister, and the most remarkable of his collaborators; for Talleyrand brought the *savoir faire* of an old-world aristocrat—brought all the force of tradition—to check the wildness of a master who was too much the self-made man. Even during the Egyptian expedition, in the dreams of the facile conquest of India or of Constantinople, we see in Bonaparte the imagination that was so dangerous when unbridled. Even during the Consulate there is an element of fancy in some of his overseas designs, if they were seriously intended; the means are not commensurate with the end. In the later years of the Empire when Talleyrand had been discarded, the Napoleonic imagination seemed to cut adrift from historic realities. But from 1799 to 1807 Talleyrand was a servant clever enough to act also as a bridle upon his master, covering Bonaparte's violence with courtesy and cunning, stealing a march on his leader by ingenious adjustments, by tricks of diplomatic delay, or by the softening of an angry phrase in an official despatch—attempting, so long as this was possible, to keep the policy of Napoleon in the channels that had been marked out by history.

It was in Germany that Bonaparte performed one of the most remarkable of the feats of his Consulate —a feat all the more remarkable in that it was the result of prestige and was carried out in time of peace. By the treaty of Lunéville of 1801 it had been agreed that those princes who had lost their lands on the left bank of the Rhine, should be compensated out of the vast aggregate of territory that was in the hands of prince-bishops, and other ecclesiastical authorities. The scheme developed into a grand territorial redistribution, and was an important step towards the simplifying of the map of Germany. In the scramble that took place for ecclesiastical lands the competitors sought Bonaparte's support and the real negotiations took place in Paris. French interests were secured as a result and they are represented in three principles that were followed in the allotment of the lands. Bonaparte increased the weight of Prussia in relation to Austria. He kept both Prussia and Austria as far as possible to the east, so that they should conflict with one another more easily than they conflicted with France. And he gave disproportionate increase—and what was still more important, a greater consolidation of territory—to states like Bavaria, Baden and Württemberg, which were near to France and were likely to come under the protection of their stronger neighbour. It was useful to have these states under special patronage as they might serve as a third group in Germany and act as the counterweight to Austria and Prussia. This whole process of secularization was a defeat for Austria, as the ecclesiastical states had tended to strengthen the imperial interest. The episode is important not only in the history of Germany but in the development of Napoleonic statesmanship there.

Although during the Consulate the court of Vienna —the court most directly affected by Bonaparte's continental policy—did not dare to renew the war that had been closed by the treaty of Lunéville, the British Government, after a year of peace, was already in a mood for further conflict. Technically we broke the treaty of Amiens, for we refused to give up Malta as we had promised—Bonaparte having been careful to carry out his engagements in this treaty, if only to rob us of any pretext for our refusal. The technical point, however, is of little importance—the real issue at stake was sufficiently avowed in the course of the controversy: whereas Bonaparte argued that his continental encroachments were not the concern of the British government, we held that we were interested in them and affected by them—we demanded compensation and guarantee. Fearing the menace of Bonaparte particularly in Egypt and the East, we refused to return Malta to the Knights of St. John; claiming it as a counter-weight to the aggrandisement of France, and as security for our communications in the Mediterranean Sea.

The impetuous nature of Bonaparte's outbursts against England, the indignities to which he subjected the British ambassador in Paris, and the haste with which he made Malta a crucial question of prestige for France were unwise—they rendered a diplomatic solution of the quarrel almost impossible. The interval of peace had been uneasy from the first—on the one hand he had complained of the protection that we were giving to the Bourbons, to royalist intriguers, to his enemies in the English press; on the other hand we had been robbed of one of our very motives for the conclusion of peace by the measures which he had taken in France against our commerce. He was retaining his troops in Holland in defiance of his engagements in the treaty of Lunéville; he had incorporated Piedmont with the French republic and offered derisory compensation to the legitimate monarch; he had secured his ascendancy in Switzerland and put a stop to English intrigues in that country. At the same time he could say that the case of Holland did not concern us—it was an Austrian treaty which he had broken. And Piedmont had been occupied by his troops before the signature of the treaty of Amiens. To Switzerland he had brought at last the blessings of peace and an admirable constitution. Here indeed the most Machiavellian feature of his policy had been his decision at a certain moment to withdraw his troops and abandon the idea of intervention—a decision which he had known would be bound to flood the country with anarchy and civil war. Perhaps we were over-anxious when he tormented us by raising our apprehensions concerning a renewed expedition to Egypt. In general we may sum up the situation by saying that England had discovered the treaty of Amiens to have been a mistake. Without asserting that Bonaparte desired to renew the war, we can insist that he was unreasonable in expecting England, in the face of his aggressions, to keep the peace. In May 1803 we retained Malta, therefore, and as Bonaparte had made its evacuation an essential point of prestige for France, negotiations were broken off. The First Consul now renewed a conflict with England that was to last until his dominion was at an end.

Bonaparte quickly extended the area that was to be involved in this conflict with England. He insisted on dragging Holland (or, as we should say, the Batavian Republic) into the war. He sent troops to occupy important ports in Naples, claiming that this was necessary in view of England's retention of Malta. He invaded Hanover and closed the Elbe and the Weser to British ships—a measure which provoked on the part of England a blockade of these river-mouths. He compelled Spain to pay a heavy tribute to France, and then to assist him in securing further tribute from Portugal; and English reprisals for these and other instances of undue compliance on the part of the court of Madrid, led to formal war between England and Spain in December 1804. From 1803 to 1805 he prepared at Boulogne, Calais, Dunkirk, Ostend, Antwerp and other ports, the grand expedition that he proposed to lead for the invasion of England. The whole of this coast was made alive with the noise of his enterprises—ship-building, harbour-construction, fortifications, trial embarkations, and the assembly and the training of what was to become Napoleon's Grand Army. Thousands of flat-bottomed boats were constructed to facilitate the landing on the British shore; and scheme after scheme was devised to enable his troops to evade the British fleet.

Bonaparte paid a number of visits to Boulogne,

and concerning these are many anecdotes highly typi
cal of the man. We hear that he was often seen gazin
meditatively at two black swans that inhabited hi
garden; or haunting a small chapel that the soldier
frequented so that he could get into conversation wit
men of the rank and file. Watching his troops drinkin
at an inn, he saw from their faces that they were bein
supplied with inferior beer. On one occasion his ey
caught an involuntary movement of the men whe
they were told to stand at ease after an exercise; i
many cases he saw the hand move to the neck and th
officers were baffled when he asserted that somethin
was wrong. When the men themselves denied tha
there was anything to complain of, he refused to b
satisfied and insisted that the men were afraid to com
plain; and he did not rest until he had proved tha
they were suffering from a uniform that chafed thei
necks. On July 19, 1804, a different type of inciden
showed to an unusual degree the violence of whic
he was capable when in anger. A naval review ha
been announced, but when the morning came Ad
miral Bruix found the weather too dangerous, an
insisted that the manoeuvres should be cancelle
When Bonaparte disagreed Bruix clung to his poin
as he was aware of the dangers of the experimen
and finally when ordered to submit he held firm an
said, "Sire, I will not obey". Bonaparte menaced hi
with his whip, whereupon Bruix, touching his swor
said, "Sire, take care". The review was undertaker
but it had hardly begun when the anticipated stor
arose; and the wreckage and the loss of life (of whic
Bonaparte showed himself not insensible) soon vind
cated the judgment of Bruix. The episode provoke

murmurs against the First Consul in places where murmuring was seldom heard.

Within a year of the outbreak of war with England a great change had taken place in the interior of France. It is now known that at least British undersecretaries and ambassadors were implicated in plots to overthrow Bonaparte and to revive civil war in France in 1803. One of Bonaparte's *agents-provocateurs,* Méhée de la Touche, discovered the threads of some of these in various European capitals. The French police ran to earth an important plot, the famous Cadoudal conspiracy, which sought to bring about a Bourbon restoration; and the opportunity was taken not merely to crush the conspiracy but to exploit it, and Bonaparte more than ever before struck terror into his enemies by one of the swift dread strokes that signalise the modern dictatorship. The Duc d'Enghien, a prince of the house of Bourbon, was virtually kidnapped on neutral territory. It was found that he had had no part in the Cadoudal conspiracy though naturally he had laboured for the overthrow of the republic. He was brought to the castle of Vincennes and given a mock trial before a military commission, when his grave had already been dug outside. Within a few hours he was shot, in the early morning of March 21, 1804—not for his sins but as a challenge to the Bourbons and as a symbol of the relentlessness with which the regime was to be maintained.

Already Bonaparte had become a virtual monarch and in his palace there had developed the ritual of a royal court. The republican character of the government had been lost already; but men were fearing for the stability of the regime. The promulgation of the

Civil Code, the development of material prosperity in France, the public works, the beautifying of Paris, had helped to magnify and consolidate the glory of Bonaparte. Splendour had become the fashion and there was a cult of the grandiose. Bonapartist propaganda capitalised the royalist plots—using them to spread fear for the durability of the regime. The moment had come for another plebiscite and the French Republic was now transformed into an hereditary empire. The intention was that Bonaparte—in case of accident—should have a successor in the government of France; but the Napoleonic imagination took hold of the matter and enlarged the whole meaning of the event; for Bonaparte adopted the insignia and sword of Charlemagne and for a moment virtually held court at Charlemagne's capital, Aix-la-Chapelle. The Pope was induced to come to Paris in December 1804 to crown the man who had so recently disposed so summarily of the Duc d'Enghien. He was given to understand that his compliance would serve the cause of religion in France, and he was able on behalf of Josephine to insist that Bonaparte's civil marriage should be completed by the religious ceremony before the coronation. At the crucial moment in the coronation ceremony Bonaparte took care to put the crown on his head himself. This is the point at which Beethoven, finding that his idol had feet of clay, angrily destroyed the dedication to Bonaparte which had been intended for the Heroic Symphony.

These events amounted to a new and serious challenge to the Habsburgs; for Napoleon did not merely change the dictatorship that he held in France into an hereditary royal office. As usual he brought history and imagination to expand the implications of his new rôle. At every opportunity he made it clear that he was determined to be nothing less than the new Charlemagne. The legitimate descendant of medieval emperors was the Habsburg ruler of Austria, Francis II; for he was the elected Holy Roman Emperor, though by no means a universal ruler now, nor—save in a ghostly sense—even the ruler of Germany. He adopted, however, an hereditary imperial title at this time, in virtue of his family possessions. Besides being Holy Roman Emperor he became henceforward, therefore, Francis I, Emperor of Austria. Napoleon's claim to be the new Charlemagne did not merely challenge shadowy antiquarian pretensions on the part of the Habsburg family. It contained within itself an implied reference to Italy—one that affected not dignity only but real dominion. This fact, combined with the presence of the English in Malta and the Russians in Corfu, made the Italian peninsula the focal point of European diplomacy in the year 1805.

Having assumed a royal title in France, Napoleon could scarcely consent to remain a mere president of a republic in the north of Italy. After he had offered the crown to two of his brothers—intending perhaps to placate Austria—he decided to possess it himself. He was careful to make the most of the situation by securing that he should be invested with the old crown of Lombardy. Instead of taking the title of king of Lombardy, he turned the old Cis-Alpine republic— recently the Italian republic—into what he now called the kingdom of Italy; alarming Naples and Austria in particular with what seemed like a claim to domination over the whole peninsula. He declared that France and Italy were to remain separate states, and that after his reign they should come under separate monarchs;

but he refused to grant the Italians the securities they most desired as a pledge of their independence. Austria was able to claim that the whole transaction violated the treaty of Lunéville which had guaranteed that independence. In addition to all this, Bonaparte had incorporated Piedmont with France in the year 1802. He now annexed the Ligurian republic, the former Genoa, to his empire, and also Parma and Placentia which for some time had been in his hands. He gave Lucca and Piombino to a sister of his, to be held as a fief of the French empire. These were clear indications of the direction of his Italian politics.

Although the Austrian army had not completed the reforms that had been intended, the court of Vienna was fortified at this moment by the conduct of other powers. The king of Sweden, the Don Quixote of the north, rampaging like a high wind, called for a coalition and a restoration of the Bourbons. The Russian czar, enraged by the shooting of the Duc d'Enghien and by the annexation of the Ligurian republic, was ready to fight on a generous impulse—to stand forward as a saviour of the weak and the missionary of a new Europe—although for the time being he himself had no urgent conflict of interests with Napoleonic France. The court of Naples had special reason for uneasiness from the moment at which Napoleon took the title of king of Italy. England was still at war, always ready to cement a continental coalition with gold.

Prussia, however, long jealous of her Austrian rival, and not yet aware of Napoleon's designs in Germany, had made peace with revolutionary France ten years before, and had found it not unprofitable to be Napoleon's friend. Prussia was still a second-rate power—

whipped for a moment only into the first rank by Frederick the Great—and it is not surprising that she was unable to achieve the masterly policy that many people expected her to pursue in this period. Her very situation imposed upon her the tactics of a rising state —the attempt to snatch what profit she could from the quarrels of her greater neighbours. She was not in a position to see in Napoleonic France a power irremediably hostile to her own advancement. She was not to know yet that Napoleon was a man who would insist on subjection even from an ally. He offered her Hanover, which he had taken from George III—the one prize he had gained in his struggle with the English monarch—while the Czar Alexander, the close friend of the Prussian king, made attempts to draw the court of Berlin into the coalition against France. Prussia reserved her final decision until the moment came when there was nothing left for her to decide.

In August 1805 Napoleon was giving his attention to the prospect of a European war. In that month Austria formally joined the coalition and decided to take the offensive, thinking to over-reach Napoleon in the important matter of time. The Austrian forces were divided, and the largest of them—under the best of the generals—was sent into Italy, though in fact the issue was to be decided in Germany; while in this latter region, the Austrian army moved recklessly to the west, too far in advance of the Russian forces that were coming to join them. The Austrian troops marched forward in this way in order to compel Bavaria to enter the alliance against France; but the Elector had already made his treaty with Napoleon and his troops managed to escape the Austrians to co-operate with the French Grand Army. General Mack, the Austrian commander, therefore had come to a dangerously advanced position to no purpose, and foolishly imagined that he was impregnable in his occupation of the fortress of Ulm on the upper Danube. Mack thought even that Napoleon would have difficulty in raising an appreciable army for the war in Germany—he would have to leave so many troops at Boulogne to repel a British invasion, so many troops also within France to deal with revolutionary movements that were expected there.

In reality, Napoleon's prestige had become dangerously involved in the project of an invasion of England. He might well have been thankful therefore for this grand digression which the war of the Third Coalition imposed upon him; thankful that the troops he had collected in the north could now be employed in an effective manner. The Army of Boulogne now became the Grand Army and marched with wonderful speed and remarkably co-ordinated movements into Germany—advancing sometimes under cover of night, the newspapers being forbidden to make disclosures concerning its whereabouts. Napoleon himself stayed in Paris until the last moment in order still further to conceal his designs. Then on October 17 a bewildered General Mack, who had believed until the last moment that his enemy was the distressed party, found himself surrounded and capitulated, leaving Napoleon to march with little interruption to the Austrian capital.

On December 2, 1805, when Napoleon was coming into difficulties in Vienna, when also it seemed that the Prussian king was on the point of joining the Third Coalition, another battle—one of the greatest of Napoleonic battles—was fought at Austerlitz. Dr. Holland Rose writes: "Never since Marlborough cut the Franco-Bavarian army in twain at Blenheim had there been a battle so terrible in its finale and so decisive in its results as this of the Three Emperors, which cost the allies 33,000 men and 186 cannon." Once again the enemies of France were over-sanguine and Napoleon predicted the mistake that they would make. He allowed them to advance against him with their left-wing until they had weakened the junction between their left-wing and their centre. Then he massed his forces against them at that point of weakness and before the day was over the Emperor and Czar were put to flight. Only the battle of Trafalgar marred the completeness of Napoleon's victory over the Third Coalition. Its consequences were serious, however, for it put an end to French sea-power during his reign.

Italy was now at Napoleon's feet, Austria had to surrender Venice and her Adriatic lands. A punitive expedition drove the Bourbons out of Naples, where Joseph Bonaparte, elder brother of the Emperor, was installed as king. From this moment Napoleon made great efforts to gain Sicily also, and his agents now became active in the Ottoman Empire. Russia began to fear French designs in Turkey, and England showed renewed anxiety for the Mediterranean. Ever since his first Italian expedition Napoleon had dreamed of empire in the Mediterranean, and from the close of the year 1805 he betrayed his preoccupation with this region—he was still fascinated by the Near East. In so far as he planned his course in advance this was the course that he began mapping out for himself for the near future. The completion of the conquest of

Italy began to appear as only a phase of a wider imperial design.

In Germany, where Napoleon now creates principalities for his lieutenants, makes marriage-alliances with princely houses, confers the regal title upon rulers of client-states, and provides further aggrandisement for Bavaria, Württemberg and Baden, the Habsburgs are henceforward a broken power. Fifteen of the German states are formed into a Confederation, the famous Confederation of the Rhine, under his protection; and in these states he gains partial control in fiscal and commercial matters, full supervision of the conduct of foreign policy, and complete command of the resources in time of war. As the rulers in his patronage refuse to recognise their obligations to the Holy Roman Empire, the Habsburgs consent to abandon a dignity that has lost all its significance.

The conduct of Prussia on the eve of Austerlitz had been so dubious, and had constituted so serious a potential menace to the French army, that the rulers of this state were bound to feel at the mercy of Napoleon when the Third Coalition had been destroyed. Prussia made the further mistake of restoring her army to a peace-footing before she had come to an arrangement with France. Bonaparte was able therefore to deal severely with her and to fasten her in nominal alliance with him on his own terms. He gave Hanover to the Prussian king and insisted that Prussia's ports should be closed to English commerce, involving the court of Berlin in hostilities with England, and thereby imprisoning it more rigidly in his own system. Prussia, the ally of Napoleon now, whether she wished it or not, thought to make virtue of necessity and gain a share in the leadership of the new Germany. She imagined that she might even control a confederation of northern states that would counterbalance the Confederation of the Rhine. Napoleon not only showed contempt for these pretensions, but opened a negotiation with George III on the basis of a restoration of Hanover; whereupon the Prussians, taken with sudden panic, imagined that he was preparing to make them his next victim. From fear, and at the same time out of a desire to challenge Napoleon for a share in the leadership of Germany, the court of Berlin began to prepare for war in the summer, and rejected the assurances that he was now only too anxious to give. They went to war exultantly as though Frederick the Great were still with them and the old efficiency of the military machine were still maintained. They marched without even waiting for the help of an ally, though the Czar was their friend and had made no peace-treaty with France after Austerlitz. They rejected repeated overtures from Napoleon who claimed that far from having designs on Prussia he had been looking to possible developments in the Near East. On October 12, 1806, they were defeated at Jena, and as their resistance collapsed their whole country was completely overrun. Nothing now could challenge Napoleon's mastery of France, Italy and Germany.

Napoleon sought to avoid congresses and general negotiations, and if he proposed them during the course of a war it would be for some tactical reason —perhaps only with the intention of producing delay. His diplomacy was facilitated by his determination always to treat separately with each of the powers which had business to transact. By this he preserved his moral ascendancy at the start, and against enemies who could be strong only by virtue of combined action he maintained a strategic position. He would take advantage of negotiations that he was holding simultaneously with separate powers—would offer the same concession to each in order to secure the *quid pro quo* from both, or would frighten one of the parties with the revelation that he was on the point of concluding a treaty with the other. In separate transactions he was better able to provoke and magnify the jealousies and the conflicts of interest which were latent amongst his enemies themselves. And it was his policy to tempt each state to be self-regarding and so to divert all of them from plans that envisaged a general European settlement. Working upon these methods he could be more sure of the emergence of those "chances" and incidents which give a surprise turn to a diplomatic negotiation; such things indeed he made it the special purpose of his diplomacy to exploit. He would meet a terrified plenipotentiary and play upon his loneliness, now threatening and bragging as if to wear down the man's resistance, now turning to moods of good humoured friendship or confidential coaxing; finally perhaps creating an atmosphere of panic by the circulation of a deliberately falsified report. The craft of diplomacy was made an auxiliary to the art of war and all its resources were used to magnify the consequences of military success.

It was further asserted by Napoleon that a given state had its range of interests, and matters extraneous to this were not to be discussed in negotiation. On this view, for example, England had no right to meddle in continental affairs save where Hanoverian objects might be in question. So there would be nobody to stand against him in the interests of Europe as a whole. A "pacification" might be reached, yet no single treaty envisaged the balance of forces, the map of the whole system, the welfare of the world. Based on partial arrangements and piece-meal transactions, such a pacification would be bound to produce more anomalies, more of the technical difficulties that he loved to exploit. One of his biographers has said: "Before the time of Napoleon there was no Europe." It is easy to see, in fact, that nothing assisted him more than the isolation of the various powers and their mutual suspicions and jealousies.

Chapter 5

Grand Empire

NAPOLEON, who would often speak of Destiny, had a curious feeling for the place of chance in human affairs. He knew how to use the moment as it came, how to co-operate with events, how to share the work with Providence. Often in his correspondence he postpones a decision, confessing that it must depend upon the course that other people take. His progress to Grand Empire which to us seems so straight and masterful, was in fact a curiously supple thing, taking its direction from the accidents of the time, conforming to the mobility of events. In the very decision that was to carry him to the conception of Grand Empire, the dream, as we shall see, did not come before the action, but afterwards. It was not the plan drawn up in advance that decided the form of the actual story; but the after-play of the Napoleonic imagination upon a situation that had already been produced. After Jena, after the sensational swiftness with which Napoleon overran the whole of Prussia, driving the king from Jena to Stettin, from Stettin to Königsberg, till he reached the farthest edge of his dominion, he found himself lord of a wider world; from a new altitude he made a new survey of his position; and, conscious that now his stature was increased, he began to change his very conception of the empire that he had achieved. He began also to find new formulas to justify and explain his aggrandisement.

It had not been his desire to have this war with

Prussia, a war which had torn him away from other preoccupations. His eyes had been drawn during the year 1806 to the Mediterranean and the Near East. A prophet in that year would have predicted that the trouble in the immediate future was likely to lie in this part of Europe. It had been the Prussians who had insisted on having a war, and Napoleon had shown petulance because they had diverted him from these other things. Now that the conquest of Prussia had been so easy, he stood with his army in what had been Poland and reconsidered his place on the map. We can actually see him trying to find what to do with his victory, how best to exploit this new advantage that he had gained. Should he exact a penalty from the king of Prussia and make peace, accepting him at his side again as a chastened and repentant ally? Should he revive the kingdom of Poland at Prussia's expense —a policy very congenial to French traditions and sentiment? Or should he refuse a treaty altogether with a landless king who had nothing left with which to negotiate—depose him, perhaps, or, failing this, hold Prussia under occupation for an indefinite time? Various alternatives were in Napoleon's mind. It was as though he was not sure what he wanted to do with the victory he had gained. The final decision was to depend on the conduct of others—Napoleon was waiting to see what the Russians would do.

The development of his imperial design comes in fact at this moment as his answer to a problem of strategy. The court of Berlin had summoned the Czar to its help and then, as we have seen, had rushed into the fight without waiting for its ally. On November 3rd it became clear to Napoleon that the Russians were advancing to meet him, whether Prussia still desired it or not. He could not afford to fight the Russians in Poland and have Prussia standing sullen and resentful in his rear. He had decided that if the Czar was coming to fight him, there could be no peace-treaty for the time being with the Prussian king. He had realised further that the same contingency would make it necessary to rouse the Polish subjects of Russia and Prussia to a national revolt. All depended on the conduct of Russia, and when that became clear, his mind was released; his decisions were ready.

It was strategic necessity, then, which, as Napoleon himself explained, decreed the continued occupation of Prussia by the French invader. The Napoleonic imagination, however, once again entered into the story to enlarge the scope of the decision. Napoleon did not declare that he would occupy Prussia until the Russian armies had been driven out of Poland. He said that the Prussian king should return to Berlin only when the English—"the eternal enemies of the continent"—had made peace with France. Moreover, since Prussia was a conquered country it should not be restored to the Hohenzollerns save in return for an equivalent; and as the Prussian king had nothing left with which to make a bargain, his lands must be redeemed by England's surrender of the conquests she had made overseas. The very fact that England was at war with France was to be the excuse for an extension of Napoleon's European dominion. And as, after Jena, by the Berlin Decree, the ports under his control were to be closed to English shipping, we begin to see towards the end of 1806 the shape of the continental design which came to its climax at Tilsit.

The Polish campaign of 1806-7 proved the most unhappy that Napoleon had hitherto conducted. The distance from France, the hardships of winter, and, when the thaw came, the depth of the mud made the waiting wearisome and the warfare indecisive. All the time an unreconciled Austria was ready, if Napoleon should come into difficulties, to take him in the rear. The French troops themselves were less contented now; they were beginning to ask if they were never going to stop until they reached China. Talleyrand was already dubious of these expanding adventures and for that very reason was being excluded from important business. Even Napoleon began to show distaste for the campaign; we find that occasionally he wrote his letters in a dejected mood. Then, when June arrived, the warfare seemed to take heart again. On June 15 the Russians were put to rout at Friedland.

Still, the loss of a battle, the defeat of one army, did not necessarily mean that the Czar of All the Russias was at Napoleon's mercy. Russia could not be reduced like other states by a swift military stroke and a direct march to the capital. Napoleon himself was too wise at this date—and the miseries of the Polish campaign were still too fresh in his mind—to permit an attempt to push his army into the heart of Russia. He had no desire to imitate Charles XII of Sweden; he was not yet blinded by the self-confidence that later drove him to Moscow. It was sufficient for him if Russia would leave him unmolested in his dominion over the rest of Europe; happiest of all if she would consent to be his accomplice.

The grand conception of the Tilsit system would seem to have been born in a Prussian mind; for the

Prussians, having put their hopes upon the Czar, and knowing the disaster at Friedland to be fateful most of all for them, imagined by a diplomatic manœuvre —by the proposal of the participation of the Turkish Empire—to divert the evils that were so gravely menacing. Since England had been neglectful of her continental allies—intent only upon the capture of sugar-islands for herself—she need not be surprised if Prussia and Russia abandoned her alliance and decided to throw their weight into the opposite scale. To desert the coalition and go into partnership with France, to seduce Napoleon by the prospect of a new and dazzling adventure, to form a syndicate for the liquidation of the Ottoman Empire—this was the scheme which it was hoped would forestall the thunders of destiny. And the Prussians brought the Czar over to this policy, coaching him in the various aspects of the design—though feeling, apparently, that Napoleon might not be so easy to convert. They were optimistic—a memorandum by the Prussian statesman Hardenberg on June 22 (three days before the first interview at Tilsit) said that the new combination "founded upon bases equally profitable to all three powers, will impose its settlement upon the rest of Europe and force even England to make an equitable peace. . . . If this system is adopted Napoleon cannot wish to weaken Prussia, on the contrary he must seek to make her strong."

They little realised how their plan would be turned to their own discomfiture, how in persuading Alexander to admit the idea of a reversal of policy they had been doing the spadework that Napoleon would have found so much more difficult to do for himself. Never was a system so torn from the hands of its makers and wrested to serve a purpose so contrary to its original one. Never were the tables more aptly turned than when the Czar who came to seduce Napoleon was flattered and charmed and finally made captive in the very net that he had brought. The two Emperors met on a raft on the river Niemen and Alexander made a mistake at the start when he attacked the conduct of his English ally. Napoleon, the dominant personality on such occasions, could work wonders with such a man in a personal interview; and it was Alexander who was unable to be merely unscrupulous—who had to throw his expansive sentimental self into the new system of policy; it was Alexander for whom the prospect of Turkish dismemberment was glamorous—Napoleon, earlier and later than this, was not attracted by such a scheme, and preferred to keep Turkey as she then was, under his own patronage, rather than share the spoils, if he could help it, with any other power. So Alexander through the brave colours of his own dreaming was bewitched and was drawn into complicity with the aggressions of France; and though the salvation of Europe from those aggressions had been his real motive in the war against Napoleon, the new romanticism drove out the old quixotry, and the face of things was blurred in the curious emotional haze that was evoked at Tilsit. Even Prussia, the Czar's particular protégé, though not abandoned, not betrayed by any act of conscious hypocrisy, was somehow overlooked—allowed to slip from the place that she had had in the original plan—so that she emerged, in spite of her subtle contrivings, the real victim of the Tilsit coup. The genuine features of the alliance that resulted were the pledges that Russia made—recognition of the French Empire, acquiescence in its further expansion, and the promise to support Napoleon if the war with England did not come to an end. The poetry of the alliance, the things which were not guaranteed in water-tight diplomatic language in the clauses of treaties, were the things that Alexander had at heart—the salvation of Prussia and the dismemberment of the Turkish Empire. On these matters it was the Czar who was the complaining party in the months that followed the signature of the treaties. And Tilsit, a magnificent setting for such a drama, saw Napoleon the dominant figure in the interplay of romanticism and ruse.

Now, when Prussia and Russia agreed to break with Great Britain, and Sweden, Portugal and Denmark were to be compelled to do the same; when even Austria could no longer stand as a neutral power, but must become an unwilling accomplice, abandoning diplomatic and commercial connections with England; when the treaties of Tilsit which put an end to the war on the continent, brought not peace but the perpetuation of conflict, the erection of crisis into a permanent system—Napoleon found himself lord of the continent, and the physiognomy of his peculiar form of dominion assumed its final shape. There was to be no more neutrality in Europe and all nations were to sigh for the return of normality, for peace with England. The war with England in fact was itself turned into the pretext for a great extension of Napoleon's domination over the continent. While it continued it was to be the excuse for prolonging a state of emergency in Europe, for keeping armies in occupation in Germany, for tightening a hold upon clients and subject-states. Treaties became operative, treaty obligations were greatly multiplied, and German principalities that had no coast-line had the Napoleonic despotism brought home to them more closely, because France could plead the existence of a state of war—because England, a shadow-enemy, was refusing to make peace.

The Continental System, the attempt to seal Europe against English commerce—the one imposing weapon that remained to Napoleon after the abandonment of the plan of invasion and the destruction of the French fleet at Trafalgar—implied a further intensification of his tyranny, a multiplication of his direct interferences, in the regions over which he possessed influence; just as by its own internal necessity it entailed the expansion of empire (demanded increasing control of the European coast-line for example) till what had begun as merely the means to an end seemed to become the end itself, the purpose which the whole Napoleonic order was directed to subserve. In the course of time Napoleon occupied Rome, drove his brother Louis from the throne of Holland and annexed the country, incorporated Hamburg and Oldenburg in his empire, and undertook the expedition to Moscow; and in all these policies he had it in mind to put a stop to leakages in his Continental System. It would be wrong to say that he conquered Europe merely because this was a necessary preliminary to the subjugation of England; for the war with England, as we have seen, had its origin, its *raison d'être,* in his policy of continental aggrandisement. The process of expansion, however, in future, the pretext for aggression, the very pattern of the structure that was formed, are conditioned by the struggle with Great Britain; so that almost we might say the Continental System becomes the fundamental basis of extended dominion—in other words, the Continental System is in fact the Grand Empire.

The object was to cripple England's exports and make it difficult for her to subsidise continental governments or keep troops in Europe; also to disturb the economic life and dislocate the financial system of the country. Lacking command of the seas, however, Napoleon was not able to intercept England's American trade; and even when the United States for a time went to war with Great Britain there was the rest of the world open to British enterprise. The Continental System did not seriously interrupt the course of the "industrial revolution" in this country; and the difficulties that arose for us in this period must be put down to that revolution, to the currency-policy of the government, to the existence of a state of war, as well as to Napoleon's commercial measures. The attempt to seal the continent against us was a thing which he himself hardly regarded as practicable, in any case. His brother, Louis, the king of Holland, made the remark that one might as well try to prevent the skin from sweating. An official in Prussia said that it would be equally feasible to order the birds to stop building their nests in the country.

At Heligoland in the North Sea, and at Malta in the Mediterranean, vast establishments were erected as bases for the smuggling of English goods. Far from being a mere risky adventure, this smuggling became a highly articulated system—a different organisation from the usual one, but still a regular organisation for a regular trade. And the system was so far acknowledged that we find Napoleon writing on the export of gin: "Fix the places where the smugglers are to come to fetch it." For the sake of the customs-duties he was willing at various times to relax his prohibitions. He argued that the government might well have some of the profit that was being taken by the smugglers. He issued licenses for trading with the enemy, on the condition that the imports from England were balanced by exports from France. But the goods taken out of France would even be thrown into the sea, since there was no sale for them in England. They would be exported at artificial valuations, purely to conform with the demands of the French Government. The book-publishers in particular released their accumulated stores, which could be bought cheaply though their ostensible price was high; and when Napoleon's agents discovered the ruse, and reduced the nominal prices of these works, books in glorification of Napoleon were collected for export across the Channel, on the assumption that the agents of the Government would not take it upon themselves to question their ostensible value. Consignments of these books, landed in England but left unsold, were shipped back to France after 1815; and the chief result of Napoleon's regulations was to increase the price of the goods that were being imported into France.

The Continental System, however, ought not to be regarded as merely a war-measure, a by-product of the conflict with England. It constituted Napoleon's economic policy—a vast preferential system in favour of France. It did something for the foundation of the cotton-industry and for the production of sugar out of beet. And it gave French industry a certain protection at a time when England was racing ahead with her "industrial revolution." The policy was one calculated to please the industrialists but to give dissatisfaction to the merchants: the Napoleonic era, as we might expect, brought about the ruin of the ports of France. Furthermore the system protected France against the rest of Europe—the rest of the Napoleonic empire. This can be realised if we glance for a moment at its effects in the kingdom of Italy.

Napoleon attempted to turn that kingdom into an "economic colony" of the French Empire, so that its raw materials should serve the interests of French industry, while its manufactures might complement where necessary, but never compete with, those of France. He encouraged the introduction of machinery into France but declined to do the same in Italy. He became jealous even if French workmen emigrated to the peninsula to give it the advantage of their technical experience. A French business man in Italy was treated as a native; an Italian in France suffered the disabilities of a foreigner. And while the peninsula was starved of raw materials or compelled to import from France alone the textiles she might require, on the other hand if France had need of Italian manufactured goods these were earmarked for her, and she was able to procure them at a lower price. Furthermore, the Continental System ruined the commerce of Italy and put a stop to ordinary commercial relations with England which had persisted until 1806. And it was not Italy who gained as a result, but France, whose exports to the peninsula showed a remarkable increase as the years went by. Ports like Genoa and Venice (and, later, Trieste) came to ruin as soon as Napoleon touched them. His wars and his territorial rearrangements robbed them of their traditional commercial channels. The kingdom of Italy suffered because parts of the peninsula, like Tuscany and the States of the

Church, were annexed to the French Empire—locked away behind tariff walls; and the last blow was struck at the prosperity of Venice when Istria and Dalmatia —so important for the commerce of that city—were made a department of France, while Venice was annexed to the kingdom of Italy.

If this was the fate of Italy which was under the direct sovereignty of Napoleon, we shall not be surprised to find that subordinate monarchs were reproved when they showed consideration for the interests of their subjects. Napoleon's relatives, the kings of Holland and Naples, for example, were resentful at times and bewailed the tyranny of their patron and over-lord. He accused them of forgetting what they owed to him—affecting to conduct affairs as though they had been born on the steps of their thrones. This was one of the reasons why Holland lost its separate status and eventually became incorporated in the French Empire. The Grand-Duchy of Berg, though it comprised a region which we should regard as one of the richest in Europe for industrial purposes, suffered greatly from the fact that it lay just outside the limits of the Empire itself—outside Napoleon's protective system.

Apart from this, the lands under Napoleon's domination suffered from the wars, the conscription, the insecurity of economic life. They were subjected to arbitrary treatment at the hands of the police, to irregular exactions and summary confiscations of goods. And Napoleon might merely use the argument from conquest as the pretext for these requisitions. On the other hand he provided roads, improved canals, abolished antiquated gilds and corporations. The very fact that he rationalized the government would open careers to talent and remove hindrances to economic development. To many states he brought the advantage of what we might call a good shaking-up—elevating men whom the *ancien régime* had tended to depress. So there remained in after years many people who never forgot the Napoleonic world and could find something in it to be grateful for, at least in retrospect. There remained veterans who looked back at times to the great days when they felt that Napoleon had given them something to live for; and longed occasionally for the exhilarating life that had spurred them to an activity beyond their ordinary powers; and would even speak as though, now that Napoleon had left the stage, history had settled down to something humdrum and meaningless again.

It was as though Europe had been lying there, a sluggish and amorphous mass, waiting for the French Revolution to bring fire and an organising principle. For well over a century that continent has suffered bitterly, and is groaning still, because too much history happened in the period between 1789 and 1815—the processes of change too wilfully congested there, and fateful movements too drastically telescoped; with cataracts, stampeding, and violent uprootings to fret and flurry the path of progress. Europe has to be plagued with monsters that the eighteenth century never contemplated, because at a crucial moment one man was brilliant enough to exhaust the possibilities of exploitation that were implicit in the system of things. Where Napoleon carried his dominion he produced or he precipitated what we might call a geological subsidence; and if we say that he only hastened historical processes that were bound in any case to have their effects in the course of time, still it was the running ahead of time that was the evil—there are things which can only be good provided they do not come too quickly. Liberalism and nationalism may be wise and enriching if they have blossomed naturally without the generation of great pressure; but we have learned now not to be happy, as our forefathers were, when sometimes these things have appeared too hurriedly and too soon. If Napoleon may claim to have carried something of the results of the French Revolution throughout Europe, if it may be said that his tyranny provoked amongst the nations movements more portentous still, we may hesitate before we count it to him as virtue that he tore his way into the ancient fabric of the European states, and so mangled the processes of historical change.

Unlike the twentieth-century dictator he turned his empire into a gigantic family interest. He looked back to the conquerors of ancient days and in his imagination power was a thing to be conceived under dynastic forms. He gave subordinate kingdoms to his relatives, attached importance to marriage-alliances with ruling houses, divorced Josephine in order to marry a princess of the Habsburg family, and was anxious to have a son who should be his successor. Throughout his system, indeed, there runs something of the Corsican feeling for the clan. His brothers proved recalcitrant and not always capable. His mother was intractable, saving her pennies as in former days, jealously alert even for any waste of firewood. She watched the prosperity of these wilful children of hers with a certain scepticism, saying: "It's all very well while it lasts." And she accumulated a great fortune against the time —which she knew was coming—when her impetuous brood would have to take shelter under her wing again. Napoleon's sisters would quarrel in public and make ugly "scenes" at court—a court in which the wife of one of the marshals, though she had once been a laundry-woman, would figure as a duchess. The descendant of Alexander and of Charlemagne loomed over a whole continent, but, though everything else might be his, grace and charm seemed to have been frightened away. He himself could not rise from a chair, could not enter or leave the room, without betraying his origin; and he kept ladies frozen with fear at his court, or offended them by a brusque allusion to what he considered to be their real function, the bearing of children. On this side he was a somewhat pathetic figure—not happy to have the appearance of a parvenu. And in marrying the Habsburg princess Marie Louise, in 1810, he may be regarded as attempting to win a hostage from history and tradition.

It is when we see him at work, however, when for example we read his correspondence, that we catch a glimpse of the greatness of the man. The variety of the problems with which he dealt in the course of a day, the speed with which his mind refocussed as it passed from one topic to another, the mastery which he displayed in the face of complexity and detail—these, and the fire of his imagination (the striking phrases, for example, that were hurled like rocks as he made his impetuous sallies, pacing the room and wearing out one secretary after another) are evidence of a personal force that has rarely been seen in the world, one that has left a lightning-streak across the pages of history. In the midst of a campaign he still governed France, issuing orders concerning some industry or rules for an educational institution. Amid letters that regulate the detailed movements of troops will come others complaining of a theatrical performance that has been permitted in Paris, or a newspaper article, or the gossip in the cafés; others that direct the style of official propaganda or review the reports of the ministers in France. Writing from the headquarters of his army he would correct an error in the report of his secret police; he would seize on a discrepancy in a complicated sheet of regimental returns; when he was fighting in Spain he remembered three fountains that had gone dry in Paris. At the same time he would be directing his diplomats, conducting for example a controversy with the Pope; or he would write disquisitions on the art of government to a refractory brother, saying: "A prince who in the first year of his reign is considered good is a prince who will be laughed at in the second." Amidst technical correspondence and official instructions we may find a letter to the Empress to reassure her concerning the weather or the state of Napoleon's health; perhaps an intervention in some quarrel between members of the family, an attempt to teach Louis, for example, how a man should handle his wife.

When he writes to the Pope he projects the problem of the moment against the background of the whole history of the relations between Church and State. He remembers that he is Charlemagne, or he is Constantine. He constructs magnificent phrases, knowing that the struggle is an epic one. At the same time he has a political theory for his own day—knows the place that he wants the Pope to occupy in the life of the world, knows the service that he expects the pulpit to give to the state. Great power can accrue to the man of action who also has a head for doctrine—one who is saved from the defects of the academic mind, but has the capacity for generalization and synthesis. Napoleon had this power—it made him a skilful propagandist—and he had also a great gift in the use of words. Telling phrases—prose not beautiful but dynamic—would come easily from him; and if when he read poetry aloud it was with the insensitiveness of one who sees poetry only as a thing to declaim, it is true also that he had a flair for the kind of prose that fits the world of action—the kind of language that an orator might love. From his correspondence—from business letters devoted to the problems of the passing day—one could glean a body of maxims that form a systematic view of the art of government. Some of these might be maxims from Machiavelli; many of them came from the application of Machiavelli's fundamental principle —they were the result of the use of a historical method for the discovery of definite points of political technique. Working not as a student but with a stateman's eye—marshalling history always to serve his purposes, imposing himself upon it, so to speak, and reading it in the light of his own experience—he was able to use history without superstition and to take lessons from the past without great danger to himself.

What is most remarkable in his letters, however, is something that is not history, and not theory, and not a world of general ideas. It is something which it is not easy to turn into continuous English, for it does not appertain to the thoughts and systems which the man had in his mind. It is a quality which was in Napoleon as a man of action, and words like energy or assertiveness or agility are too weak to describe it. He once said that when he made one of his great decisions, it came to him as though he had just remembered something. He also said that when he travelled in new country he would entertain himself with the military problems it presented—storing his mind in advance with all the possible situations. We have watched him already at times waiting upon events, and holding alternative courses of action in his mind, realising that the situation is a moving one, and that he must retain his elasticity. Then, when the signal has been given—when, for example, the enemy has shown his hand—all the appropriate decisions are waiting in readiness; the pressure of the proper button gives them instantaneous release. He was a strategist in the sense that the mathematician is a strategist when he solves in the space of a few lines a problem upon which a mediocre man would squander twenty sheets of paper. There is economy, there is the glamour of a swift swoop, there is—if one can forget the cruelty—a high aesthetic thrill, in that trenchant daring stroke, that quick adaptation of means to ends. And instead of the retardation which purpose so often seems to suffer when passing from thought to action, he took that transition, so to speak, with gathering speed, collecting more of himself into the idea as it turned into action; as though the very exercise of will, the very fever of contest, were an exhilaration to him.

From the time of the treaties of Tilsit his character shows more obviously than before the corrupting effects of unbridled power. Even court amusements, we are told, were blighted by the fear that men had of their Emperor—a person whom Talleyrand called "inamusable," and who failed to realise that human beings cannot be made to laugh by mere word of command. From this time it would appear that in European relations he imagined himself to be above any need for diplomacy, above the race of men who have to conduct policy by way of mutual transaction. He bullied, he issued commands and rattled the sword, forgetting to be diplomatic even with his ally, the Czar of Russia. And because the Pope allowed loopholes for English commerce, he destroyed the Temporal Power, "revoked the Donation of Constantine," as he said, and made himself master of Rome. Talleyrand is a good barometer, and he moved away from Napoleon at this time; he declared the cause of the Emperor to be separable henceforward from the interests of France. His successor in the ministry of foreign affairs was Champagny, who was nothing more than a subservient tool.

Typical of this unskilfulness of Napoleon after Tilsit is the fact that in 1808—having made use of the Spaniards in his conquest of Portugal—he managed to put his troops in occupation in Spain and send his brother Joseph as King to Madrid. The Bourbon government in Spain has been weak; its abuses had been flagrant; but Napoleon confessed later that he had been wrong at this moment in failing to cover his high-handedness with a better screen of diplomacy. With curious spontaneity risings broke out in town and village as though a grand synchronised movement had been arranged; and though Napoleon could defeat in formal battle any army that the Spaniards were able to put in the field, Spain is suitable for guerilla warfare—raiding bands could harass the communications and make regular government impossible. And as he himself once said, even a Napoleon cannot be everywhere at once. This Spanish resistance provided England with a foothold on the continent, and under Wellington we were able at last to come to grips with the enemy. The constant trouble that Napoleon had in

Spain—and the fact that he was unable to give this region his undivided attention—created what he came to describe as a "running sore" and encouraged his other enemies at times in the thought that they might over-reach him while he was in difficulties. The effectiveness of a popular rising—a grand ebullition of a whole nation—against the tyrant, even led to a new theory of resistance, a new valuation of the spirit of nationality. The very force which had made France great was now being turned against Napoleon himself. We may say that by 1808 the summit of his power has been reached.

Chapter 6

Moscow

ONLY a large-scale biography could demonstrate the multiple activities, the jostling crowd of inter-connected problems, the cascade of enterprises, adventures and decisions, which the Napoleonic empire entailed; or could give the due impression of Napoleon as one who (whether in politics or in war) continually disposes large masses, directing the complicated movements of the inter-related parts—one who, conducting an army, for example, maps out the separate routes for each division, timing their respective journeys so that they punctually converge. In this slight sketch we have seen a little of what might be called the mechanics of Napoleon's rise to power; we have watched something also of that process which, by observable transitions, brought him to the conception of Grand Empire; we have missed, however, the cumulative effect of the detailed narrative, the impression of multiplicity, and perhaps still more, the impression of mass. We might turn now to observe how in 1809 the Habsburgs went to war with Napoleon again, resisting more obstinately than ever, but finally submitting to his terms; how meanwhile, the Pope had been hustled out of Rome—captured by French soldiers at the break of day and ("without time even to do his beard" one of them wrote) carried away in a locked carriage; how at the close of that year Josephine was divorced, and when Napoleon had decided upon this action he could not eat his dinner but made a tinkling noise on his glass—

reaking the dreadful silence only to ask an officer the ime, and then seeming not to listen for the answer. But life, unlike art, is riotous and redundant; and history is so rich that she can afford to waste herself. We who can only bring an occasional light upon the past must pick and choose—not pretend to tabulate all the battles of Napoleon's campaigns. The structure of the story, the essential situation as we have studied it in outline, remains the same, though nature must play many variations on the theme, and sing the same song twice over, before a new stage of development has been reached. We must merely say that, with the scene disposed roughly speaking as we have observed it, with Napoleon's Continental System operating still, and carried even to a higher power, England in the years 1810-11 is driven to crisis, discouragement and distress.

It remains to us now, therefore, to look at the next stage in the process—the downfall of a dictatorship. And because we are not concerned with the vicissitudes of states, but merely with the figure that one man has made in history, we must look particularly at the Moscow campaign, which, if it does not add to the portrait, enlarges the shape that Napoleon projected across Europe. We must examine this campaign not merely because of its historical results, but because it is a significant section of life that he had to traverse. We may regard it as an essential chapter in the epic of Napoleon.

It must not be imagined that for any length of time the Russian alliance retained the glow and the assurance of the Tilsit days; though for a period it achieved its principal purpose, the immobilising of the possible European enemies of France. The

Czar, when he returned to St. Petersburg, found complainants even amongst his relatives, who were ready to say that he had been duped; and in the spring of 1808 he was becoming importunate—had Napoleon forgotten his promises? A further interview at Erfurt proved necessary in order to confirm him in his new system of policy; and this time the monarchs of Europe, the satellites of Napoleon, were in attendance— it was a grand pageant of the Napoleonic empire. Napoleon himself admitted, however, on this occasion, that he found Alexander already a changed man. When Austria went to war with Napoleon again in 1809 the Czar gave it to be understood that though ostensibly an ally of France he would avoid doing the court of Vienna any material harm. Napoleon knew of his duplicity and even suffered as a result, but had his revenge in the peace-treaty when the Austrians had been defeated. The Russians became jealous of the favour he showed to the Poles, jealous even of his relations with Austria. Shy of giving him a Grand Duchess themselves, they were unhappy when he married a daughter of the Habsburg Emperor. Finally, since they suffered cruelly through the trade restrictions, the Czar began to withdraw from the Continental System—and this caused an important leakage at the very time when Napoleon was tightening the system and beginning to see a chance of success. In 1810 it was being realized that the breach was approaching; and at the close of that year Napoleon annexed the Duchy of Oldenburg which belonged to the brother-in-law of the Czar. Some of the Russians were ready for war in 1811. Napoleon, who always held that the first sign of weakness would release all the latent hostility with which he knew he was surrounded, was committed a hundred

imes over to his Continental System. In 1812 he had
gathered together a Grand Army which was an aston-
shment even in that age of military prodigies.

On Tuesday, June 23, at two o'clock in the morn-
ng, he was examining the banks of the Niemen near
Kovno to find a suitable crossing for his army—he and
his attendants having made an exchange of uniform
with some Polish cavalrymen. At this point there was
only a ferry to serve the high-road that came from
Königsberg and went forward to Vilna; but, having
chosen his crossing at a bend in the river above Kovno,
Napoleon had three bridges constructed, about 300
yards apart. Elaborate dispositions were made for the
passage of the army; it was evidently expected that the
Russians would defend the entrance to their territory.
No resistance came, however, and on the Wednesday
and Thursday the Grand Army made a splendid cross-
ng under a glorious sun. For two days Napoleon remained in the little town of Kovno, making arrangements for more bridges in his rear, for river transport
up the Vilia from Königsberg, for hospitals and stores,
and for the ovens that were so urgently needed. In the
meantime his army was pressing on to Vilna, the old
capital of Lithuania, where he himself arrived at about
noon on the Sunday.

It was a town of dark and dirty streets with not
more than 25,000 inhabitants. These included many
Jews whose condition (according to one writer) "did
nothing to brighten the picture." It was situated on the
Vilia, a river "which winds through the country in vain
and does not seem to fertilise it." The convents were
very numerous. There was a great cluster of domes
and steeples. Since the first partition of Poland Lithu-

ania had been Russian, and now, after forty years, th
French were apparently greeted as deliverers. It
possible, however, that the inhabitants welcome
Napoleon in the hope of inducing him to make th
military occupation more lenient. He was fêted an
gave audience to the University; and Polish flags wer
now mounted on the walls. He stayed eighteen days i
Vilna organising an important depôt there, and mov
ing up supplies from Königsberg. And there he inte
viewed Balashov, an emissary from the Czar, an
rejected what he knew to be the last possibility o
negotiation. He teased Balashov by commenting o
the number of churches that he saw; but when he sai
that piety was out of date he received the disconcertin
reply: "Not yet in Spain and Russia." And when h
inquired the way to Moscow, affecting the style of
tourist who was proposing to visit the place, Balasho
was bold enough to pay him in kind and said: "Ther
are many routes. Charles XII came via Pultusk."

Already the French army was in difficulties. It ha
marched too hurriedly to Vilna in the hope of forcin
an engagement. 10,000 horses, according to one ob
server, had been left lying in the road. On June 29
heavy storm arose and for five days the rain continue
ruining the roads and disorganising the transport
Pillagers were already becoming the scourge of Lith
uania and in the first week of July some offenders wer
shot in the public square at Vilna. All the while Nap
leon was waiting anxiously for news from his broth
Jerome who commanded an army on the right. "Yo
are jeopardising the success of the whole campaign
he wrote; and in truth, the great object of his origin
manœuvres was being lost at this very time. He him
self had made the initial mistake in giving the com

mand to Jerome and in directing movements when too far away from the scene of operations. Jerome could not move quickly enough to prevent Bagration in the south from uniting with the main Russian army further north. Furthermore Napoleon refused to commit himself to a reconstitution of the kingdom of Poland at a time when national fervour had been kindled in Warsaw. The co-operation of the Poles became more doubtful as a result. He appointed a provisional government for Lithuania but it soon appeared that this was a mere cover for military exploitation.

On July 16 he left Vilna at 11 P.M. He travelled more by coach than on horseback now, but a lantern in the rear of the coach enabled him to work at night. When he came to a halt and found a lodging he would first have his maps, papers and books laid out on tables, or if necessary on planks supported by trestles; but if he was entering a town from which the Russians had retreated, then, having given a few essential orders, he might ride ahead for a few miles to reconnoitre—always looking for a battle. On the 19th he learned that the Russians had decided not to make a stand in their entrenched camp at Drissa. On the 23rd he was hoping that they would defend Vitebsk and he wrote: "We are on the eve of great events." Still on the 28th he was on horseback in the early morning (having bivouacked in the midst of his troops) expecting to find "a second Friedland." But even at Vitebsk the Russians withdrew before him, and from this moment the prospect began to appear more forbidding. At Vitebsk, the capital of White Russia, an attractive town of 25,000 inhabitants, he was forced to halt again. He had overpressed the march, and it was clear that his exhausted troops must have a rest.

The troops had hurried forward, but provisions were delayed—diarrhoea, dysentry and typhus had begun to spread amongst the soldiers. Of the 150,000 horses that had been brought it is reckoned that half the number had been lost by this date. Many of the troops, especially the foreign contingents, were straggling, deserting, pillaging the country. Comparatively few had been lost in battle, yet 120,000 men had already disappeared.

The horrors of the winter that supervened have dimmed the memory of the scorching heat of July and August. Napoleon himself was more than ordinarily fatigued by it; "never before had he found his clothing so wearisome." In Vitebsk he would undress and lie on his bed, and (what was unusual in him) even receive officers without troubling to put on his uniform. It was light enough at 10 P.M. to read a letter, we are told, and as light again at two o'clock in the morning. But sometimes, and particularly after a thunderstorm, the night would turn cold; and one man reported than on July 1 "we had to light fires." On the other hand the rain would be disastrous for communications. And, after a storm, if the road was made only of logs that lay across a marsh, the horses would displace the timbers, and, falling into the interstices, break their legs.

At Vitebsk he takes over convents for use as hospitals, organises supplies and reviews his troops. The problem of stragglers requires his attention. He makes careful inquiries about the route to Smolensk. He orders the destruction of the entrenched camp behind him at Drissa, lest it should be useful to the enemy in the event of a return journey. He remembers that Paris needs news, that pamphlets must be circulated amongst the Poles, and he writes to Laplace: "I have received your treatise on the theory of probabilities with great pleasure. . . . The advancement and perfection of mathematics are clearly bound up with the prosperity of the state." After executing a brilliant manoeuvre intended to turn the Russian lines (only, the enemy in these days has learned to be ready for his devices) he sees Smolensk, a place of special sanctity in the eyes of the Russians—a city with thick walls and numerous towers, and with cupolas, gilded and painted, rising picturesquely amid trees. Wastefully he throws his troops into a direct attack upon the Russians, for he must have a battle. But bitter as it is, it is only a rearguard action; the Russians are marching away when he enters the town on the 18th. Most of the inhabitants had fled and much of the town had been destroyed by fire. The French could not deal with their 15,000 wounded, and we are told that gun-wadding and the parchments of the city archives had to be used for bandages.

In Smolensk on the 21st he seems to have made the decision to go forward—to go, if necessary, to Moscow; and perhaps if we consider the state of France and of Spain behind him, the problem of unwilling allies and restless subject nations, we may feel that a man like Napoleon could have chosen no other course. In his initial proclamation he had described this enterprise twice over as merely "the second Polish campaign." He had not originally envisaged it as the Moscow campaign, though he seems to have told Murat that he would be in Moscow next year and in St. Petersburg the year after. For both military and political reasons, however, it was important not to halt until he had won a victory and established his

prestige. As yet no one foresaw irretrievable disaster
In Russia there was discontent amongst the people
there was bitter quarrelling amongst the generals. And
every few days, as they drew back, the Russian army
seemed to stand and prepare for battle, and then re
treat again as though in search of a better ground.

Marching in dust and heat, the French pushed for
ward; but everything behind them was in terribl
confusion. They had to live to a great extent by
marauding but in the track of the Russian army ther
was a great waste so that the marauding had to exten
for many miles. Now more than ever Napoleon wa
preoccupied with the problem of the length of hi
communications. He established a new base at Smo
lensk, arranged for the government and defence o
that region, summoned more troops up from the Nie
men to guard the rear, and inquired into the garrison
of captured towns, now open to Cossack attacks
More bridges and ovens had to be constructed an
it was necessary to order that men coming up from
Smolensk should make parties of five or six hundre
at least, because of the danger from parties o
Cossacks. And foraging had to be organised, becaus
under the existing lack of system the Russians, sai
Napoleon (speaking wildly perhaps), made hundred
of prisoners every day.

Often we see him grumbling now. He railed, fo
example, at Berthier, his chief of staff, calling him a
old woman and offering to send him back to Paris
When anybody ventured to offer an objection on som
point or other, he would say, "So you, too, are on
of those who have had enough of it." The bulletin
that he issued at this period are remarkable in thei
mendacity. He was "avid for information" and ha

amusing interviews with Russian stragglers who had
fallen into his hands. On September 2, bad news having arrived from Spain, he wrote at length to Paris,
criticising the conduct of Marmont whose defeat at
Salamanca had entailed the abandonment of Madrid.
By this time a battle with the Russians was imminent,
however, and though there was an alarm one night
when it appeared that the fires in the Russian bivouacs
were going out, the battle took place at last near the
village of Borodino.

Forces which at the crossing of Niemen had been
300,000 strong, numbered only 120,000 when they
faced the Russians at Borodino; and of these almost
a third were killed or wounded in the course of the
battle, and the rest were dispirited if not demoralised.
Since it was not sufficient to turn the Russian lines
and open the way to Moscow, since Napoleon's aim
was to meet and break the enemy forces, he had ordered a direct attack upon the position the Russians
had chosen, a position which they had improved by
defensive works. And once he had made his initial
arrangements he could do little more than watch the
course of events; as one writer has said, when the
start had been made "the battle fought itself." At this
supreme moment he had a severe cold—we find him
writing a bulletin because he was unable to dictate it
—and he seems to have been genuinely unwell; but
though there are complaints of his listlessness behind
the lines, Marbot mentions that he was in a position
to receive reports from various parts of the field, and
adds that "an icy wind, blowing with great force,
prevented him from staying on horseback"; while it
does not appear that his illness affected his dispositions
for the battle—wasteful though they were of human

life. His refusal to send his Guards, his last reserve, into action, when they were demanded, is scarcely open to criticism. The Russians, driven from the Great Redoubt which was the centre of bitter conflict, retreated after the battle, but they were neither broken nor demoralised. Napoleon could not be sure that they would allow him to enter Moscow without attempting another resistance.

It was Napoleon's view that Destiny laid a hand on him and drew him to Russia. He afterwards seemed to think, perhaps not entirely without justice, that in going to Moscow, even to meet tragedy, he had somehow increased his grandeur. It was as though he felt that he would have been a smaller historical figure—less wild a thing for men to wonder at—if he had given way, consenting to half-measures and mean adjustments, in which in any case he had no faith at this point in his career. He had the art of seeing himself silhouetted against the horizon—seeing himself a figure of destiny realising the shape that he would make in history. Far from being the master of the course of his own career he knew that he was a partner with fate, and that events themselves made decisions for him. In going to Moscow, as we have seen, he was making the same response to the same kind of necessity to which he had always bowed. He did not pursue his course in mere exultant confidence but with anxieties and forebodings. Perhaps if he had not fought the Czar he was still a beaten man—it is easy to be too dogmatic on the point. He might bluster—it was his task to inspire confidence—but once when he said to Rapp, "Don't you realise that I have a star," the general still noticed that "his face bore the marks of disquietude." At any rate as we watch him

move to Moscow we may feel not that he was glori-
ously defying Providence, but that he was cheerlessly
following his fate, not knowing whether it led to triumph or overthrow; and we may think that rarely has
so much human life been spent, not for the sake of
the state, but in fulfilment of one man's destiny.

Soldiers who had seen the Pyramids and the Alps,
Berlin and Vienna, Rome and Madrid now took heart
again as they came to the goal of this their most fateful chapter of wandering. The scenes at this point of
the story are so vivid that they have become part of
the familiar furniture of our minds—Napoleon gazing
from the Sparrow Hills and exulting at the prospect
of domes and towers, of churches and palaces in
Moscow; then staying the night in a hovel in the sub-
urbs, with vermin in his bed and the smell so intolerable that he would call to his valet, "Are you asleep,
Constant?" and, since Constant could not sleep either,
would add, "Very well, my boy, burn some more
vinegar"; then the procession that should have been
a triumphal entry, only there was no one to surrender
the keys of the city, no throng of spectators, no faces
at windows, "not even a pretty girl listening to regimental bands"; and the silence was sinister, as though
this were the parody of an entry into some city of
the dead. Then, the following night, when Napoleon
was as the Kremlin, there were the fires that started
up in so many parts of the city, while a gale was
blowing and the wind was apt to change direction—
Napoleon himself (his hair singed and his coat scarred
by the fire) having to move to a palace outside the
city, walking along narrow streets, littered with
charred wood and splintered glass—the flames from
each side joining overhead and the fire roaring like

the din of a neighbouring waterfall. Then the return
to the Kremlin when the fire had died down, after it
had driven many of the wretched inhabitants out of
their cellars, and Napoleon is silent amongst his old
associates in these days, he dawdles at meal-times now,
and he gazes at the crows which fly over Moscow, fly
over the Kremlin itself, like an evil portent. And all
the while the French soldiers, with the loot of palaces
and bazaars, concoct fantastic costumes and gamble
for luxury wares, possessing a superfluity of confec-
tionery and preserved fruits, but not enough meat and
not too much flour. And discipline is being relaxed.

Napoleon spent three nights in drawing up regulations for the Comédie Française in Paris. He criticised
the over-interference of the censor at home, who, he
said, should take no action unless the question of
obscenity or the internal tranquillity of the state called
for the exercise of restraint. He wrote to his librarian:
"You do not send new books sufficiently punctually.
Send new publications more regularly." It was necessary to make Frenchmen think that he was reigning
serenely as a conqueror, able to give part of his mind
to things like these. He called troops forward from
Europe and demanded further contingents from his
allies; summoned more conscripts from France and
Italy, and ordered 14,000 horses from various parts
of the continent. On his arrival in Moscow he had
written to the Czar: "I have made war on your Maj-
esty without animosity. A note from you before or
after the last battle would have stopped my advance
and I would have wished even to forgo the advantage
of an entry into Moscow." This note, however, and
other tentatives during the following month, were

without result; for once the enemy could not be forced to make peace.

To stay in Moscow might prove disastrous. All Europe was waiting to take advantage of the first blow to Napoleon's prestige. It would seem that there was sufficient food for the troops themselves, but by the end of the winter all the horses would have been dead. Napoleon played with alternative plans—a march to St. Petersburg, a withdrawal upon Smolensk combined with a threat to St. Petersburg, a manœuvre against the Russian forces which had moved to the south of the city—anything that would not be rumoured through the length and breadth of Europe as a direct retreat. His marshals would listen to no talk of a threat to St. Petersburg, however, and in these days he could not afford to ignore their opposition. On October 19 (five weeks after his entry into the city) Napoleon left Moscow, intending to make a movement to the south—a detour via Kaluga—before returning for the winter to Smolensk. Great care was taken to ensure that this march should be reported as an advantageous manœuvre, not a retreat.

Within very few days, however, the march had to assume the form of unmistakable retreat. A fierce battle at Maloyaroslavetz on the 23rd left the French certainly in possession of the field; but in a hut not far away Napoleon had to survey the situation afresh and sat for an hour brooding over the map while his marshals waited for him to break the silence. On the following day he himself narrowly escaped capture by a band of Cossacks. The army moved back to the route by which they had marched to Moscow in the summer, a region devastated by the passage of two armies already—the path of direct retreat. Back across the field of Borodino they went, through the ruins of burned villages, and along roads already lined with the litter of earlier marches; and they dragged their guns so long as their horses lived, and carriages that contained precious booty from the city of Moscow, though as they proceeded they had to throw away "valuable candelabras, antique bronzes, priceless paintings and porcelain," and you heard the sound of ammunition-waggons having to be blown up in the rear. It was retreat, but not yet unmitigated disaster. Napoleon felt able to pick up 1,500 of the men wounded at Borodino and they were carried on available vehicles.

Already food was becoming scarce, however, "and the man who was lucky enough to possess bread crept off to eat it in secret." Early in November it was a starving ill-clad horde, that was creeping forward, eating horse-flesh, while the slowness of the transports held up the rear. From this point the countryside was devastated, and there was nothing left of the provisions brought from Moscow. Towards the end of the first week in November the weather, tolerable hitherto, even brilliant at times (though the nights were severe) became extremely cold. The snow began to fall, and Napoleon took to wearing fur. "The wind filled the forests with its terrible whistling and uprooted the black fir trees covered with icicles, which fell to the ground with a crash." From this date the morale of the retreating army disappears; though men look to Smolensk as the end of the journey, a place of abundant stores. At the same time Napoleon heard bad news from home. On November 6 he learned of a conspiracy in Paris and it revealed the precariousness of his position. It had been based on the fiction that he himself was dead; but, even granted that, he was shocked that no thought had been given to the young son Marie Louise had borne him. The military news from the wings was equally disconcerting—the Russian army of the Danube was marching up, and Saint-Cyr was being driven from the Dwina—two enemy forces, therefore, were closing in to bar the retreat. It was impossible to remain long in Smolensk, where Napoleon himself arrived on November 9; and here, in any case—a great disappointment—there were provisions only for a few days. Soldiers "camped in the middle of the streets and some hours afterwards were found dead around the fires they had lit." Finally, when Napoleon reached the Berezina with 25,000 demoralised soldiers and 40,000 non-combatants, the Russians were there, and after a minor engagement, the bridge at the village of Borisov was destroyed. Four hundred engineers, standing sometimes up to their shoulders in water that was beginning to freeze again, had to construct two bridges higher up the river, making use of timber from the houses of a neighbouring village—Napoleon watched the while from a heap of logs, supervising the work and regretting that only a few days before he had ordered the destruction of the pontoons. From the 26th to the 28th the crossing was made, but on the 28th there was fighting on both sides of the river. A congested mass of non-combatants took panic on one of the bridges and the other collapsed from the weight of its burden. Finally both bridges were destroyed before all the stragglers had crossed, in order to secure Napoleon's rear. On December 5th the Emperor himself left the army, telling the men that he could do more for them in Paris than by sharing their march. He left the command in the hands of Murat, the king of Naples (and the husband of his sister) but under his leadership the Grand Army melted away.

The alliance of Russia, Prussia and Austria against Napoleon—this was the combination which it had hitherto been impossible to produce. This, however, and the rising of the peoples appeared as a sequel to the retreat from Moscow. At this stage the picture re-shapes and forms itself into masses and the portrait of Napoleon is submerged. We are spectators, now, of the great unrolling, and it is no longer biography— it is the whole history of Europe that is in question; a history that would require panoramic display. Napoleon was the disciple of Machiavelli who had studied the science of usurpers, of "new princes" who arise and carve out kingdoms for themselves. He knew that the hereditary monarch is safe if he but follows the ancestral usages of his house; a new prince, however, must make no mistakes—he requires great skill and the co-operation of fortune if he is to keep his throne. Now, when the Czar decided not merely to defend his territory but to march forward into Germany; when the Prussian king, driven by a virtual uprising of his people, consented to become a partner in the alliance against France; when Austria, after delaying for a season (since Metternich saw the strength of his position and meant to gain, whichever party proved victorious) finally threw in her lot with the coalition—now, Napoleon was to confirm the truth of his forebodings, and we can see why he always appeared so self-confident in distress and difficulty, why indeed he had to appear self-confident. The first reverse, the first sign of weakness was bound to place his whole system, so to speak, on an inclined plane; and descent would take place with gathering speed, ending in landslide, the ground itself giving way beneath his feet.

His brother-in-law Murat proved untrustworthy, negotiated with the enemy, and played a game of his own in Italy. Napoleon wrote to him: "Surely you are not one of the people who imagine that the lion is dead. If you are working on this assumption you are wrong. . . . The title of king has driven you out of your mind." Already a Napoleonic marshal who had been imposed upon Sweden—Bernadotte, the founder of the present royal house of Sweden—had joined the coalition in return for the guarantee of the Swedish throne and the promise of Norway. Then Bavaria, after she had renewed her vows of fidelity, went over to the enemy, and after the Battle of Leipzig in October 1813—which necessitated the retreat to the French frontier—the Confederation of the Rhine collapsed. Forces that had hitherto been on Napoleon's side did not retire from the war, but went over to swell the ranks of the enemy. Before this, the German troops in Napoleon's armies had been deserting him, and the population had become unfriendly. Now, even when he summoned troops from Italy, they melted away before they arrived, no longer content to fight for France. Still he showed his accustomed energy— recruiting vast new armies, clothing, equipping and training these with remarkable speed, and working eighteen hours a day. He tried also to move about in Paris, and even attend the theatre, systematically inspiring confidence. When he presented colours to young soldiers and then suddenly turned on them and cried: "You swear to guard them?" the fire and fervour came—he could still cast a spell over his troops. In Germany the allies sought to defeat him by attacking his lieutenants, drawing back whenever he himself appeared. And his final defence of Paris showed him as brilliant as in former days—he could still say: "I am the one who can save France, not you." All around him, however, the sands were giving way, now that he had lost all his allies, now that enemies were converging upon him from east, south and north, now that subject-states were in revolt. Paris was riddled with intrigue, and first among the conspirators was Talleyrand, his old associate, working for a restoration of the Bourbon monarchy. Ministers had lost heart, agents were devoid of energy, marshals were sullen; and in the Corps Législatif men who had been subservient hitherto began to talk of liberalism and of Napoleon's "intolerable tyranny." In the atmosphere of defeatism men said that France was invaded only because the Emperor had refused to make a reasonable treaty. "If he were dead we should have peace," it was whispered. And if the lower classes were faithful, the bourgeoisie—those whose sons had evaded earlier conscriptions, but could no longer escape—were ready for a new regime. Finally, when Paris had been captured (March 30, 1814) and Napoleon was contemplating a further prosecution of the war, his marshals—some of those who had not actually deserted—opposed the idea: "We must not risk turning Paris into another Moscow," they argued. Since his lieutenants persisted in their opposition he declared that he would do without them, he would lead the army himself. "The army will refuse to march," said Marshal Ney. "The army will obey me," the Emperor replied. Ney answered, however—and this was most tragic of all—"The army will obey its leaders"; and Napoleon did not challenge the fact.

He abdicated and attempted to poison himself. When he was restored he took the recovery as a decree of fate. Moving across the south of France to the island of Elba, which the allies had conceded to him, he was greeted with curses in Orange, his carriage was stoned, and at Orgon men shouted "See the odious tyrant." If he had not borrowed disguises from the troops of the foreign enemies of France, he might have lost his life.

Chapter 7

Two Final Scenes

FOR TEN MONTHS Napoleon stayed in Elba, in the miniature dominion that had been conceded to him. Some of his enemies pressed for his removal to a more secluded place; and he even feared that there were plots for his assassination. The Bourbons were refusing to pay him the 2,000,000 francs a year that had been stipulated for him in a treaty. He knew that France was restless under her restored monarchs—that the country was even ready to rise again. At 9 P.M. on Sunday, February 26, 1815, he set sail under a brilliant moon and a starry sky, and with over a thousand soldiers. Journeying to the French coast he put the best writers amongst the soldiers to the work of copying out proclamations in long-hand. To some who were doubtful about the prospect of reaching Paris without firing a shot, he pretended that an insurrection had already broken out in the capital.

They landed safely near Antibes but a detachment that was sent to win over the garrison of the town was captured and disarmed. Avoiding the disastrous region by which he had travelled on his way to Elba in the preceding year, Napoleon chose a mountain-route, where he could count on the population—purchased mules with some of the treasure which had been brought, and abandoned the four cannon which had originally been intended only to make the expedition look more imposing. One of the mules, crashing down a precipice, lost most of its burden of treasure (300,000 francs in gold) in the floods and snows beneath. Confronted by troops near Grenoble, Napoleon boldly advanced, and opening his coat, said, "If any one of you wishes to kill his general and emperor, let him do it; here I am." This was the first critical encounter, but the soldiers refused to fire and cried "Vive l'Empereur." At Grenoble, where the commander had the keys and was preparing for flight, so that it was necessary to set to work to batter down the heavy gate, Napoleon had no sooner installed himself in his hotel, than the wreckage of the gate was brought to him with the message: "They wouldn't give you the keys, so here's the door itself." At Lyons there was wild exultation and Napoleon played the monarch again, declaring that the Bourbons were deposed; and when he left this city on March 13 he had an army of 14,000 men. He came to Mâcon and reproached the inhabitants because they had opened their gates to the enemy the year before; but they blamed their leaders—"You had given us such a bad mayor," they said; and he replied: "True enough. We've all made mistakes. Let's forget about them now." After he had left Mâcon it is narrated that two peasants went to his inn and bought the bones of the chicken he had eaten, to keep as souvenirs.

Marshal Ney—who had pressed so firmly for the abdication—might vow that he would bring Napoleon to Paris in an iron cage, but he could not ignore the acclamation the man was receiving, and he could not even have confidence in his own rank and file; so that when Napoleon, always able to strike the note that would challenge the loyalty of an old soldier, sent a letter of forgiveness to him, Ney quickly returned to the service of his Emperor. "I have no doubt, that when you heard of my arrival in Lyons," the letter ran, "you made your troops hoist the tricolour again. Carry out the orders that you get from Bertrand and come to meet me at Chalon. I shall receive you as I did after Borodino." The defection of Ney meant the removal of the last great obstacle and the Bourbons and their court now fled from the capital. When Napoleon reached Paris on the night of March 20 the palace of the Tuileries was ready for him—"from the kitchen-staff to the grand-chamberlains," his servants and his court had prepared for his reception. According to a soldier who caught sight of him when a door was opened, he went to rest in a chair, with his feet on the mantelpiece, for he was very weary and had eaten nothing all day.

And yet this fair fabulous adventure, this consummate escapade—product of bluff and hazard that came near to perilous regions of rarefied poetry—only ended by providing a story for the world to wonder over—as though Nature, just to be prodigal, had intended merely to show that the trick could be done again. For Napoleon himself the end of the journey brought only anxious second thoughts. Even at Lyons he had heard "Down with the Bourbons," "Down with the priests," and he had caught the underlying note—the love that Frenchmen had for the Revolution. The France which now acclaimed him was a different France, and he knew that for the time being he would have to pay some attention to the liberals. He might say that France had need of his "right arm," he might protest that "France is looking for me but does not find me," he might claim: "I am not a military despot but the peasants' Emperor, I represent the people of France"—the words seemed ominously shallow now. While he still hoped for peace in Europe he promised concessions to the party of reform. Later, at St. Helena, he said of this period, "I made a mistake in losing most valuable time by troubling myself with the question of a constitution." "Those wretched liberals wasted my time," he repeated; and though he granted a House of Representatives and freedom of the press he was insincere. In any case the concessions were only sufficient to whet the appetites of the men with whom he had to deal. He would have been involved in constitutional difficulties even if his foreign enemies had left him at peace. Once it was known that there was to be war against Europe—and the *rentes* fell from 80 to 57—he regretted that he had so far committed himself in the direction of liberalism.

In the Vendée the royalists rose in rebellion. In Europe the enemies of Napoleon drew more tightly together, declared war, and decreed his outlawry. "An Austro-Sardinian force threatened the south-east of France. Mighty armies of 170,000 Russians and 250,000 Austrians were rolling slowly on towards Lorraine and Alsace . . . 120,000 Prussians under Blücher were cantoned between Liége and Charleroi; while Wellington's composite array of British, German and Dutch-Belgian troops, about 100,000 strong, lay between Brussels and Mons." Instead of waiting for his various enemies to converge upon him, Napoleon assumed the offensive, hoping to separate Wellington and Blücher. Not without mishaps over which he brooded long in after-years, not without mistakes over which historians have had copious controversy, he led his army into the Low Countries and finally came to his Waterloo.

They sent him to St. Helena, and on this occasion he departed as a prisoner; but he had begun to see himself as something of a martyr and he threw his imagination into the rôle. The man who read Voltaire's *Charles XII* while he was waiting in Moscow—and when his hopes were rotting—had the quality which in a journalist we call *flair*, and he knew at the end how to manage his own publicity. Even in his downfall, therefore, he was able to secure for himself (what he so greatly prized) the silhouette against the sky. In one respect it is not too malicious perhaps to say that his enemies gave him the punishment that fitted the crime; for the man whose dreams had been so grandiloquent was condemned to peevish controversies and little-mindedness. In the close circle of his own handful of followers, emotional crises were intensified, personal jealousies constantly arose. Between Napoleon and his captors there was an unattractive feud—the one side apprehensive of the intrigues of the Frenchmen, the other side erecting complaint into a system and deliberately multiplying grievances for purposes of propaganda. Precautions that were taken to prevent his escape—curtailment of his evening walks, attempts to keep him under observation—gave colour to his complaints. The use of the title "General Bonaparte" and the refusal to forward books addressed to the "Emperor Napoleon" offended a man who was particularly sensitive on these points. He knew how to exploit the situation and we find him attempting to convince the world, for example, that he was forced to sell his silver plate in order to provide his little party with food.

Here in St. Helena he dictated his Memoirs, assembling for the purpose such printed materials as were then available. The men around him would take notes also of his conversation, in order to have their own records to deliver to the world. So the Napoleonic Legend (which has its antecedents in mendacious bulletins, in the propaganda of earlier years and in some of the declarations after the return from Elba) was carefully elaborated; and everything was done (in Napoleon's will for example, and in his suggestion of a constitution for the reign of his son) to surround the Legend with the convincing attendant circumstances and give colour to its claims. As this was a Legend, moreover, concerning not the past so much as the future, not Napoleon's deeds so much as his secret intentions and his ultimate principles, it had a certain degree of plausibility; especially in view of the fact that it was directed to a Europe restless under the Reaction, rebellious under the system of Metternich. According to the propaganda from St. Helena, the veritable Napoleon had never been able to reveal himself. All the policies of the historical Napoleon had been emergency policies in a desperate time of war. At heart he had been a liberal, a lover of nationalities, a friend of peace and of the Catholic religion, and the apostle of the "United States of Europe." The malice of other powers had dogged him perpetually, however, forcing him to fight to defend his régime and to preserve the achievements of the Revolution. "I asked for twenty years and destiny only gave me thirteen," he said. When he became Emperor, France was not yet ready for liberty, he claimed: "96 Frenchmen out of every hundred were illiterate." Neither was Germany in a condition to be unified—he would have installed three great monarchies there, combined them in a federative system, and provided compensation in the Balkans for the princes who had been dispossessed. When we turn to the *Journals* of the frank, uncourtly Gourgaud we can judge of the insincerity of these protestations: "The King of France is too liberal, he will lose his crown." "France needs a sceptre, needs firm government, needs to be ruled with an iron hand." "If I had won [at the battle of Waterloo] I would have turned the Chambers into a laughing-stock."

He would say sometimes that he believed in God —"The greatest minds have believed, not merely Bossuet, whose business it was, but Newton and Leibnitz who had no interest involved." Sometimes we might imagine him an eighteenth-century deist, but one who possessed a sense of the sublime, a capacity for awe, a feeling for the mystery of a starry night. Man had need of the supernatural, he said—"better find it in religion than go looking for it in a Cagliostro"; but since no single creed was as old as the world he would examine them all and regard them with relativity; urging, however, that it was a good thing to hold the religion of one's country, and die in the faith in which one happened to have been brought up. He was capable of the remark: "If I had to have a religion I would worship the sun, which gives life to everything. The sun is the true god of the earth." But there are moments when men feel like that; and we need not make heavy weather of a confession of this kind. It was Napoleon's way to throw in an extra remark, a gratuitous discrepancy, to disconcert us at the finish; but if we allow ourselves to be plagued by the mystification we are falling into just the trap that he loved to set for the chroniclers who were to come afterwards.

He died on May 5, 1821, having previously received extreme unction. He was buried in his green uniform at St. Helena, under two weeping willows that stood in a valley. He had asked that his ashes should rest by the side of the Seine, and in 1840 his body was removed to Paris. By this time Louis Napoleon had become active. A new chapter in the history of Bonapartism had begun.

Bibliographical Note

A. GENERAL WORKS (mostly procurable in English)

An admirable biography for students and general readers who require a full and scholarly account of Napoleon is the work by August Fournier: *Napoleon I. Eine Biographie* (Vienna and Leipzig, 1886-89), which has been translated into English by A. E. Adams (2 vols., London, 1911).

The Life of Napoleon I, by J. Holland Rose, first published in 1902 (11th edition, revised, London, 1934, 2 vols. in 1) was an important contribution to the study of this period and incorporated new material from the British Record Office. It presents what may be called the British view of the Napoleonic wars and still holds its place as the most important biography of Napoleon produced in this country.

An excellent brief study of Napoleon by H. A. L. Fisher can be obtained in the Home University Library.

In the series *L'Histoire de France racontée à tous* Louis Madelin has produced two considerable volumes on *Le Consulat et l'Empire* (Paris, 1933), and the first of these has appeared in an English translation in the corresponding series: The National History of France (London, 1934). This work is based upon a long and profound study of the period and is written in an easy narrative style, though it contains some provocative judgments which (at least as yet) have not been definitely substantiated. The larger history which M. Madelin promised in the course of the above-mentioned work is *Histoire du Consulat et de l'Empire* in 16 volumes (Paris, 1937-54).

Those who are interested in having a portrait of Napoleon or a picture of his mode of life rather than a formal biography may care to consult:

Frédéric Masson: *Napoleon at home* (English transl.,
2 vols., London, 1894).

Arthur Lévy: *Napoléon intime* (Paris, 1892).

J. Holland Rose: *The Personality of Napoleon*
(London, 1912; cheap edition, 1929).

The *Itinéraire général de Napoléon Ier* by A. Schuermans (Paris, 1908) and the later work, Louis Garros, *Itinéraire de Napoleon Bonaparte, 1769-1821* (Paris, 1947) enable the reader to discover where Napoleon was and what he was doing at a given date.

B. Works and Correspondence of Napoleon

The *Correspondance de Napoléon Ier* was published by order of Napoleon III (1857-70), but though the letters down to 1815 ran to 28 volumes and numbered over 22,000, the work was incomplete and many supplementary volumes of correspondence have appeared under various editors since 1870. A list of these collections can be found on pp. xiv and xv of: *Napoleon I: Letters,* selected, translated and edited by J. M. Thompson. (Oxford, 1934.) Other selections in English are:

A Selection from the letters and despatches of the First Napoleon, edited by the Hon. D. A. Bingham (3 vols. London, 1884).

New Letters of Napoleon I, translated by Lady M. Loyd (London, 1898).

Letters and Documents of Napoleon, selected and translated by J. E. Howard, of which Vol. I has appeared (London, 1961) reaching May 1802.

For the early writings of Napoleon see:

Frédéric Masson et Guido Biagi: *Napoléon inconnu. Papiers inédits.* 1786-1793 (2 vols. Paris, 1895).

Henry Foljambe: *Napoleon's notes on English History made on the eve of the French Revolution* (London, 1905).

C. WORKS ON SPECIAL TOPICS for students who desire
   further reading on particular episodes or seek the
   grounds of particular interpretations that have been
   put forward in this book:

CHAPTER 2. THE RISE OF BONAPARTE

A. Chuquet: *La jeunesse de Napoléon Iᵉʳ* (3 vols.
   Paris, 1897-99).

On the antecedents of Napoleonic warfare, Spenser
Wilkinson: *The French Army before Napoleon* (Oxford,
1915) gives a brief account. J. Colin: *L'éducation mili-
taire de Napoléon* (Paris, 1900) is a work for students.
G. Ferrero: *Aventure* (Paris, 1938), which has just appeared in English under the title *The Gamble,* is a viva-
cious, perhaps over-coloured account of the new type of
warfare as it was exemplified in the Italian campaign of
1796-7—eminently a book for the general reader.

A. Mathiez: *Le Directoire* (Paris, 1934) for the coup
   d'état of Fructidor.

François Jules Charles-Roux: *Bonaparte; governor
   of Egypt* (English transl., London, 1937).

CHAPTER 3. FIRST CONSUL

Vandal: *L'avènement de Bonaparte* (2 vols. Paris,
   1903; cheap edition, *Collection Nelson*) for the
   coup d'état of Brumaire.

On the internal history of France and the organisation
of government under Napoleon, see G. Pariset: *Le Consulat et l'Empire,* 1799-1815 (Paris, 1921); Vol. III in
Lavisse: *Histoire de France contemporaine.*

Pierre Villeneuve de Janti: *Bonaparte et le code civil*
   (Paris, 1934).

CHAPTER 4. THE PROGRESS OF AN IMPERIAL DESIGN

The diplomatic history of France in the Napoleonic period has been closely studied in a series of works by M. Edouard Driault—e.g. *Napoléon et l'Europe: La politique extérieure du premier Consul,* 1800-03 (Paris, 1910). These works are an important contribution to the technical study of Napoleonic diplomacy as it is revealed in the documents at the French Ministry of Foreign Affairs; but they are for students rather than for the general reader, and in some of their wider interpretations they are open to controversy. One of them, *La Politique orientale de Napoléon,* 1806-8 (Paris, 1904) is of importance to those who desire to arrive at an interpretation of Napoleon's policy in the Near East.

> Geoffrey Bruun: *Europe and the French Imperium, 1799-1814* (New York and London, 1938), in the series entitled "The Rise of Modern Europe," edited by Wm. L. Langer.
>
> Georges Lefebvre: *Napoleon,* in the "Peuples et Civilisations" series (3rd. edition, Paris, 1947).
>
> H. A. L. Fisher: *Napoleonic Statesmanship: Germany* (Oxford, 1903).
>
> Albert Pingaud: *Bonaparte: Président de la République italienne* (Paris, 1914).
>
> E. Driault: *Napoléon en Italie* 1800-12 (Paris, 1906).
>
> H. C. Deutsch: *The Genesis of Napoleonic Imperialism* (Cambridge, Mass., 1938).
>
> Henri Welschinger: *Le Duc d'Enghien: L'enlèvement d'Ettenheim et l'exécution de Vincennes* (Paris, 1913).

On the breaking of the Peace of Amiens see:

> P. Coquelle: *Napoleon and England* 1803-1813 (Eng. transl. London, 1904).
>
> O. Browning: *England and Napoleon in* 1803 (London, 1887).

CHAPTER 5. GRAND EMPIRE

H. Butterfield: *The Peace-Tactics of Napoleon 1806-08* (Cambridge, 1929)—on Tilsit.

Eli F. Hecksher: *The Continental System: an economic interpretation* (Oxford, 1922).

E. Tarlé: *Le blocus continental et le royaume d'Italie* (Paris, 1928).

CHAPTER 6. MOSCOW

H. B. George: *Napoleon's Invasion of Russia* (London, 1899).

E. Foord: *Napoleon's Russian Campaign of 1812* (London, 1914).

H. Belloc: *The Campaign of 1812 and the Retreat from Moscow* (London, 1924, cheap edition, 1931).

CHAPTER 7. TWO FINAL SCENES

The Hundred Days—Henry Houssaye: *The return of Napoleon* (Eng. transl. London, 1934).

St. Helena—Lord Rosebery: *Napoleon: the last phase* (London, 1922).

Frédérick Masson: *Napoleon at St. Helena,* translated by L. B. Frewer (Oxford, 1949).

P. Gonnard: *Les origines de la Légende napoléonienne* (Paris, 1906).